HOUGHTON MIFFLIN

Reading

Ready Reference

Grades 3–6

HOUGHTON MIFFLIN

Printed in China

ISBN: 978-0-547-13410-9

1 2 3 4 5 6 7 8 9-LEO-17 16 15 14 13 12 11 10 09 08

Table of Contents

Ready Reference

Welcome to *Houghton Mifflin Reading Ready Reference*

Why You Need this Book

As you explore your revised *Houghton Mifflin Reading, Medallion Edition* you will find a variety of new materials designed to enhance your classroom and help meet the needs of a variety of learners. *Houghton Mifflin Reading Ready Reference* provides a wealth of support for a variety of instructional needs in an easy-to-use location.

Turn the page and you will discover:

- Instructional Routines
- Corrective Feedback
- Support for Vocabulary Development
- Academic Language Support
- Support for Struggling Readers
- Support for English Learners
- Support for Advanced Learners
- Support for speakers of African American Vernacular English
- Assessment Information
- An Overview of Writing

This is only a small part of the huge wealth of information this reference provides.

Keep it close by for Theme 1. Have it available for Theme 2. By Theme 3 your classroom will be filled with routines that make learning manageable and productive for everyone!

Use this book to plan, use this book to teach, and use this book to build on your own excellence in the classroom. You make the difference. We help show you how!

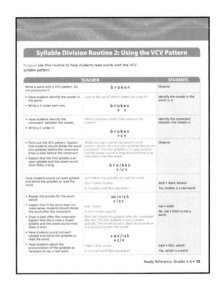

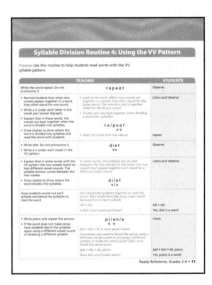

Instructional Routines

The Houghton Mifflin Reading You Created

If you are reading this, *Houghton Mifflin Reading* is probably very familiar to you. Over the last few years you and your students have become familiar with its wealth of literature.

You have your plans in place, your activities selected, and you know the parts of this program that mean success.

These pages are designed to thank you for your limitless support and to introduce you to what's new in *Houghton Mifflin Reading, Medallion Edition.*

Let's begin with the issues you told us were most critical.

Writing

The new *Houghton Mifflin Reading, Medallion Edition,* provides daily writing instruction that supports your California Standards. We asked you to show us how it should look. What you see below is the result of your design.

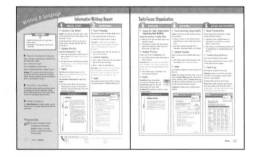

Write Source

A Book for Writing, Thinking, and Learning *Write Source* presents the writing process, traits, and forms to help students build the skills they need for writing success.

Vocabulary

We know that students must start early to develop the vocabulary knowledge that leads to a rich and useful written and oral vocabulary.

The materials that you see below represent a few of the ways *Houghton Mifflin Reading* is providing more vocabulary support than ever.

Vocabulary Readers   Vocabulary Development Lessons

The new Houghton Mifflin **Vocabulary in Context Cards** bring vocabulary to life with visuals and a complete routine for vocabulary building. They are an instant hit with students and teachers, so we created them in a size that fits everyone. Whether they are part of a work station, of a learning center, or of whole-group vocabulary instruction, teachers will find them an indispensable part of their classroom from day one!

Building Vocabulary Flipcharts build vocabulary and comprehension and provide differentiated opportunities for practice and application.

New Products to Explore

Curious About Words

Curious About Words provides **intensive oral vocabulary** support for students in kindergarten through third grade. The two Read Aloud Big Books at each grade level are a great beginning for the daily instruction designed to build oral vocabulary as well as future reading and writing capacity.

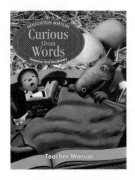 

Houghton Mifflin Reading Toolkit

The Houghton Mifflin Reading Toolkit provides intervention instruction for the five critical areas of reading. The 450 lessons give teachers the resources to support a huge number of reading skills for those students who need an extra boost.

Portals Intensive Intervention

The Portals Intensive Intervention program can be used in place of the core program at grades 4–8. Six levels of materials correspond to standards in grades 1–8. Assessment tools help teachers know when students need Portals, and when they are ready to rejoin the core.

English Language Development System

English Language Development for California provides an additional hour of daily instruction to ensure mastery of the ELA Content Standards.

Visit your theme Teacher's Edition for *Houghton Mifflin Reading, Medallion Edition* to find more on Practice Readers, Vocabulary Readers, and new Reading in Science and Social Studies Flipcharts.

Creating a Successful Classroom

Classrooms come in all sizes and shapes and tend to have a personality as unique as the children they nurture. There are certain steps that make creating a successful classroom both easier and more rewarding. These pages are designed to remind you of some of the things that can help make your *Houghton Mifflin Reading* classroom run more smoothly.

Use Routines Early and Often

If you are reading this book you have a head start on the first and most critical part of any successful classroom: building routines. This book is designed to help you locate and build the type of routines that make a classroom both student-friendly and academically successful. Keep this book close at hand. Choose a few key routines and begin them early. Add to those routines each month. Effective teachers know that routines make all the difference.

Build Awareness of Instructional Goals

Children learn more when they are directly involved and clearly understand their own goals and objectives. As many California teachers know, building a Focus Wall is one of the best ways to make this happen. Above you will find just one example of how a focus wall may be constructed. A Focus Wall brings meaning to instruction and should be updated weekly.

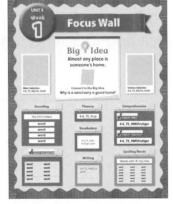

The Student Standards Handbook, found in the *Houghton Mifflin Reading* Pupil Edition, is a constant reminder of the California Standards for both Students and Families. This handbook can also be found online.

Provide a Variety of Reading Experiences that Motivate

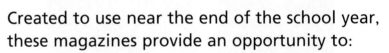

Motivation is a part of any successful venture. Classrooms may be the best example of this. In that spirit, Houghton Mifflin has created the student magazines you see pictured at right.

Created to use near the end of the school year, these magazines provide an opportunity to:

- Read high-interest materials that we hope children might select on their own

- Review critical reading skills and strategies essential to success as they move to the next grade

- Apply writing and critical thinking skills to more motivating real world settings

In addition to the magazines, Houghton Mifflin has chosen three quality pieces of literature at each grade level to support this motivating unit. This literature is a rich example of fiction and nonfiction. It also represents varying levels to allow all children the opportunity to participate and enjoy! Finally, this entire unit of magazines and literature at grades 3–6 is available in Spanish.

Novels

Grade 3

Donovan's Word Jar
Struggling Reader: Realistic Fiction

Jake Drake, Know-It-All
On-Level: Realistic Fiction

Capoeira
Advanced: Informational text

Grade 4

Justin and the Best Biscuits in the World
Struggling Reader: Realistic Fiction

Phineas L. MacGuire... Gets Slimed!
On-Level: Realistic Fiction

Sea Turtles: Ocean Nomads
Advanced: Informational text

Grade 5

Skunk Scout
Struggling Reader: Realistic Fiction

Frindle
On-Level: Realistic Fiction

Mysteries of the Mummy Kids
(Advanced): Informational text

Grade 6

Esperanza Rising
Struggling Reader: Historical Fiction

Brian's Winter
On-Level: Realistic Fiction

Tracking Trash: Flotsam, Jetsam, and the Science of Ocean Motion
Advanced: Informational text

Magazines

Grade 3: Make Your Mark

Grade 4: Paths to Discovery

Grade 5: Journey to Discovery

Grade 6: Respect and Protect

Communicating with Family and Caretakers!

Parents, caretakers and friends are the first stage of learning for any child and continue to be critical to the learning process. Communication with those supporting at home is essential to building a successful classroom environment.

Parent letters help extend learning beyond the classroom setting. Students should be encouraged to use vocabulary, practice reading skills and strategies, and discover new reasons to read at home. The materials pictured below are only one part of continuous communication between the home and school environments.

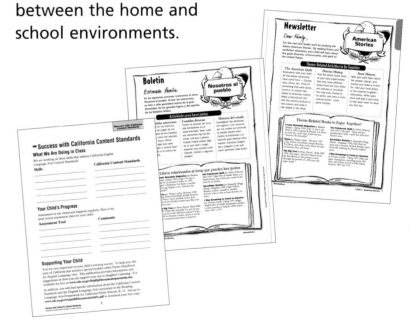

Notes

Instructional Routines

Instructional routines are activities or procedures that are predictable because students have learned how to carry them out. Routines are a basic component of successful classrooms. In fact, research indicates that the use of well-established routines is a major difference between the practice of expert teachers and that of novices.

Many routines are focused on classroom organization; these may include routines for lining up, turning in homework, and asking for assistance. Instructional routines are focused on establishing regular and predictable procedures for achieving academic goals. Some of the benefits of using instructional routines include:

- Routines save classroom time, because students know the procedure and don't have to spend time learning it.

- Routines help students organize their time and focus their effort on the learning objective.

- Students know what is expected of them, and what they need to do to be successful.

- Students feel secure when using routines they know. This reduces anxiety and helps maintain an orderly learning environment.

- Routines reduce the number of disruptions from students asking for help.

- Routines encourage students to take responsibility for their work.

These characteristics of routines help you focus on important objectives and help students achieve independence and success. They are beneficial for all students, and often are especially helpful for students who are struggling.

Routines must be taught. Students need to have the steps of a routine explained, and they need the opportunity to see it modeled and to practice it. Successful teachers take time at the beginning of the year to introduce a few important routines and to make sure that students practice until each routine is established. Other routines are gradually added as needed during the year. It may take several weeks for some routines to become well established. However, once students know how to use a routine, the benefits in saving classroom time and in enhanced learning are well worth the initial effort.

Instructional Routines

Instructional Routines for Phonics and Decoding

The following routines support instruction in Phonics and Decoding. Use them whenever they are referenced in a lesson to deliver explicit and systematic instruction. You might also use them during small-group instruction, or share them with other adults who work with your students.

Page	Routine	Use these Routines for
11–13	**Blending Routines 1–3** • Sound-by-Sound Blending • Continuous Blending • Vowel-First Blending	• Phonics lessons on Blending • Small-group instruction for Extra Support or Challenge
14–17	**Syllable Division Routines 1–4** • Using the VCCV Pattern • Using the VCV Pattern • Using the VCCCV Pattern • Using the VV Pattern	• Phonics lessons on Syllabication • Small-group instruction for Extra Support or Challenge

Blending Routine 1: Continuous Blending

Purpose Use this routine to provide children with an intermediate strategy as a transition between sound-by-sound blending and reading words with automaticity.

TEACHER		STUDENTS
Display letter cards or write letters.	m a t	Observe.
Blend the sounds, stretching out the word while pointing to each letter in a sweeping motion.	*Listen:* m a t → mat	Listen.
• Together with students, blend the sounds and pronounce the word. • Have students blend the word with you, and again on their own.	*Blend the word with me:* m a t → mat *Now you read it.*	mat mat
Repeat with more examples.	*Let's blend some more words:* f a t → fat b a t → bat	fat fat bat bat
For additional practice: • Write the words on the board and have students read them first silently, then together. • Point to words randomly and have students read them. • Choose individuals to use the words in sentences.	*Look at the words on the board and blend them in your head.* *Now read them together.* *Can you use this word in a sentence?*	bat fat mat hat cat sat

Instructional Routines

Blending Routine 2: Sound-by-Sound Blending

Purpose Use this routine to teach students a strategy for decoding unfamiliar decodable words using the English Sound/Spelling System on their own.

TEACHER		STUDENTS
Display letter cards(s) or write the letter(s) for the first sound in the word. Point to the letter(s) as you say the sound, and have students repeat it with you.	*Listen:* /m/ m *Now you say it:*	/m/
Write or display letter card(s) for the next sound in the word and repeat the procedure.	*Listen:* /ă/ m a *Now you say it:*	/ă/
Blend the sounds, sweeping your hand below the letters. Have students blend the sounds with you.	*Listen:* /m/ /ă/ m a → *Now you say it:*	/m/ /ă/
Repeat the process for the remaining sounds, one at a time.	*Listen:* /t/ m a t → *Now you say it:*	/t/
Model how to blend the whole word, pointing to the letters in a sweeping motion as you blend the sounds. Have students blend the word.	*Listen:* /m/ /ă/ /t/ m a t → mat *Now you say it:*	/m/ /ă/ /t/, mat
Tell students to use the word in a sentence.	*Make up a sentence with the word* mat.	Say sentences with *mat*.

Blending Routine 3: Vowel-First Blending

Purpose Use this routine to provide additional support to children who have difficulty with the other two types of blending and need to focus on the most important part of each word, the vowels.

TEACHER		STUDENTS
Write or display letter cards for the vowel sound in the word. Point to the spelling as you say the sound, and have students repeat it with you.	*Listen: /or/* or *Now you say it:*	*/or/*
Explain that when you come to this spelling as you blend the word, you will remember to say that sound.		
Write or display letter card(s) for the first sound in the word. Point to the spelling as you say the sound, and have students repeat it with you.	*Listen: /f/* f *Now you say it:*	*/f/*
Blend sounds, sweeping your hand below the letter. Have students blend the sounds with you.	*Listen: /f/ /or/* f or → *Now you say it:*	*/f/ /or/*
Repeat the process for the remaining sounds, one at a time.	*Listen: /k/* k *Now you say it:*	*/k/*
Model how to blend the whole word, pointing to the letters in a sweeping motion as you blend the sounds. Have students blend the word.	*Listen: /f/ /or/ /k/, fork* f or k → *Now you say it:*	*/f/ /or/ /k/, fork*
Tell students to use the word in a sentence.	*Make up a sentence with the word* fork.	Say sentences with *fork*.

Instructional Routines

Syllable Division Routine 1: Using the VCCV Pattern

Purpose Use this routine to help students read words with the VCCV syllable pattern.

TEACHER		STUDENTS
Write a word with a VCCV pattern. Do not pronounce it.	napkin	Observe.
• Remind students that each syllable has a vowel sound. • Have them identify the vowels. Write a *V* under each one.	*Look at the word. Which letters are vowels?* napkin v v	Identify the vowels in the word: *a, i.*
• Have students identify the consonants between the vowels. • Write a *C* under those consonants.	*Which letters are consonants that fall between the vowels?* napkin vc cv	Identify the consonants between the vowels: *p, k.*
• Point out the VCCV pattern. • Explain that students should divide the word into syllables between the two consonants. • Draw a slash between the two consonants in the word and between the *C*s in the VCCV pattern. • Point out exceptions such as digraphs *(bushel)*, r-controlled vowels *(barber)*, and final consonant plus -*le (maple)*.	*When you see a vowel-consonant-consonant-vowel pattern, divide the word into syllables between the two consonants.* nap / kin vc / cv	Listen and observe.
Point to the first syllable, and remind children that a closed syllable ends in a consonant, and often has a short vowel sound.		
• Have students sound out each syllable and blend the syllables to read the word. • Have students adjust the pronunciation of the syllables as necessary to get a real word.	*Let's blend the syllables to read the word.* /năp/ • /kĭn/, napkin *Repeat the word a few times to make it sound natural, napkin, napkin.*	/năp/ • /kĭn/, napkin napkin, napkin

Syllable Division Routine 2: Using the VCV Pattern

Purpose Use this routine to help students read words with the VCV syllable pattern.

TEACHER		STUDENTS
Write a word with a VCV pattern. Do not pronounce it.	b r o k e n	Observe.
• Have students identify the vowels in the word. • Write a *V* under each one.	*Look at the word. Which letters are vowels?* b r o k e n v v	Identify the vowels in the word: *o, e.*
• Have students identify the consonant between the vowels. • Write a *C* under it.	*Which consonant letter falls between the vowels?* b r o k e n v c v	Identify the consonant between the vowels: *k.*
• Point out the VCV pattern. Explain that students should divide the word into syllables before the consonant. Draw a slash before the consonant. • Explain that the first syllable is an open syllable and the vowel sound most likely is long.	*When you see a vowel-consonant-vowel pattern, divide the word into syllables before the consonant. The first syllable is an open syllable and the vowel sound is long because there is no consonant after the vowel.* b r o / k e n v / c v	Observe.
Have students sound out each syllable and blend the syllables to read the word.	*Let's blend the syllables to read the word.* /brō/ • /kən/, broken *Is it a real word that you know?*	/brō/ • /kən/, broken Yes, broken *is a real word.*
• Repeat the process for the word *vanish*. • Explain that if the word does not make sense, students should divide the word after the consonant. • Draw a slash after the consonant. Explain that this is now a closed syllable and the vowel sound most likely is short. • Have students sound out each syllable and blend the syllables to read the word. • Have students adjust the pronunciation of the syllables as necessary to say a real word.	va / n i s h v / c v /vā/ • /nĭsh/ *Is /vā/ • /nĭsh/ a word?* *Then let's break the syllable after the consonant like this. The first syllable is now a closed syllable. The vowel sound is short because there is a consonant after the vowel.* v a n / i s h v c / v /văn/ • /ĭsh/, vanish *Is it a real word that you know?*	/vā/ • /nĭsh/ No, /vā/ • /nĭsh/ is not a word. /văn/ • /ĭsh/, vanish Yes, vanish *is a word.*

Instructional Routines

Syllable Division Routine 3: Using the VCCCV Pattern

Purpose Use this routine to help students read words with the VCCCV syllable pattern.

TEACHER		STUDENTS
Write a word with a VCCCV pattern. Do not pronounce it.	p a n t h e r	Observe.
• Remind students that each syllable has a vowel sound. • Have them identify the vowels. Write a *V* under each one.	*Look at the word. Which letters are vowels?* p a n t h e r v v	Identify the vowels in the word: *a, e.*
• Have students identify the consonants between the vowels. • Write a *C* under those consonants.	*Which letters are consonants that fall between the vowels?* p a n t h e r v c c c v	Identify the consonants between the vowels: *n, t, h.*
• Point out the VCCCV pattern. • Explain that a VCCCV word has a consonant pair and is divided into syllables either before or after the consonant pair. • Ask students what the consonant pair is and draw a slash between the syllables.	*Words with a vowel-consonant-consonant-consonant-vowel pattern have consonant pairs. Divide the word into syllables either before or after the consonant pair, keeping the consonant pair in the same syllable. What is the consonant pair in this word?* p a n / t h e r v c / c c v	Listen and observe. *The t and h are the consonant pair, a digraph.*
• Have students sound out each syllable and blend the syllables to read the word. • Have students adjust the pronunciation of the syllables as necessary to say a real word.	*Let's blend the syllables to read the word.* */păn/ • /thər/, panther*	*/păn/ • /thər/, panther*

Syllable Division Routine 4: Using the VV Pattern

Purpose Use this routine to help students read words with the VV syllable pattern.

TEACHER		STUDENTS
Write the word *repeat*. Do not pronounce it.	r e p e a t	Observe.
• Remind students that when two vowels appear together in a word, they often stand for one sound. • Write a *V* under each letter in the vowel pair (vowel digraph). • Explain that in these words, the vowels are kept together when the word is divided into syllables. • Draw slashes to show where the word is divided into syllables and read the word with students.	• *Look at the word. When two vowels are together in a word, they often stand for the same sound. The vowels e and a together stand for the long e sound.* • *Vowel pairs are kept together when dividing a word into syllables.* re / p e a t v v • *Read the word with me*, repeat.	Listen and observe. *repeat*
• Write *piano*. Do not pronounce it. • Write a *V* under each vowel in the VV pattern.	p i a n o v v	Observe.
• Explain that in some words with the VV pattern the syllables are divided between the two vowels because the two vowels stand for two different vowel sounds. • Draw slashes to show where the word divides into syllables.	*In some words, the syllables are divided between the two vowels. In this word, the two vowels that appear together each stand for a different vowel sound.* pi / a n / o v v	Listen and observe.
Have students sound out each syllable and blend the syllables to read the word.	*Let's blend the syllables together to read the word. The **i** might have the long vowel sound because it is an open syllable.* /p/ /ī/ • /ăn/ • /ŏ/ *Is this a real word you know?*	/p/ /ī/ • /ăn/ • /ŏ/ No, /p/ /ī/ • /ăn/ • /ŏ/ does not make sense.
• Write *piano* and repeat the process. • If the word does not make sense, have students blend the syllables again using a different vowel sound or stressing a different syllable.	pi / a n / o v v /pī/ • /ăn/ • /ō/ *is not a word I know.* *Sometimes you need to blend the words using a different vowel sound or stressing a different syllable to make the word sound right. Let's blend this word again.* /pē/ • /ăn/ • /ō/, *piano* *Does this word make sense?*	Listen. /p/ /ē/ • /ăn/ • /ŏ/, *piano* Yes, piano *is a word.*

Instructional Routines

Instructional Routine and Activities for Vocabulary Development

Use the materials and routines below to support *Houghton Mifflin Reading* Vocabulary Development lessons. These lessons, materials, and routines provide the following important elements of rich and robust vocabulary instruction.

- initial exposure using a student-friendly definition

- discussion about the word and its meaning

- sorting, classifying, and other activities to deepen understanding of word meanings

- reading and hearing words in different contexts

- using words in different contexts, spoken and written

- visual support for English learners

Page	Routine Name	Use with...	Materials Needed
19	**Context Card Routine**	Vocabulary Development lessons	Context Cards
20–21	**Activities for Vocabulary Development**	• Vocabulary Development lessons • Small-group vocabulary lessons • Independent practice	list of Vocabulary words

Context Card Routine

Purpose Use this routine to help students deepen their understanding of vocabulary words.

TEACHER		STUDENTS
• Display the Context Card. • Read and pronounce the word. • Discuss phonics and structural cues including sound/spelling patterns. • Read the word together with students.	*Listen: create.* *Now say it with me: create.* **create** Some artists **create** things out of junk. This statue was made from recycled trash.	*create*
Read aloud the explanation under *What Does It Mean?* on the back of the card.	*When you create something, you make it.*	
• Have students read aloud the sentence on the front of the card. • Point out any Spanish cognates. • Ask how the picture and the sentence together tell more about the meaning of the word.	*Some artists create things out of junk. This statue was made of recycled trash.* *The Spanish cognate of create is crean.* *What do the picture and the context sentence tell us about the word?*	Sample response: *To create something is to make something new.*
• Read aloud the section called *Think About It* on the back of the card. • Have students use the word in sentences that suggest its meaning.	*What would you like to create?* *Now use the word in a sentence.*	Responses will vary. Sample response: *My aunt created an amazing new dessert called chocolate-cherry cream pie.*
• Give partners or small groups one or two Context Cards. • Help students, as necessary, as they begin working on the *Talk it Over* activity on the back of their cards. • Have students complete the activities for all of the cards during the week.	**create** **What Does It Mean?** When you **create** something, you make it. Spanish cognate: crean **Think About It.** What would you like to create? **Talk It Over.** Decide whether these sentences make sense. Explain your reasons. • We can **create** a skyscraper out of blocks. • The children will **create** pennies at the fish store. • My father and I **create** pancakes for breakfast. • Lions **create** sandcastles at the beach.	(optional) Record the activities in vocabulary notebooks.

Instructional Routines

Activities for Vocabulary Development

Use these activities to give your students additional exposure to Vocabulary from main selections or Vocabulary Development lessons. Select the activities that work best with each week's words and are best suited to your students' abilities. Multiple exposures and active engagement with new vocabulary helps students build greater word consciousness, and develop a richer, more robust understanding of new words.

Confounding Definitions

With a partner, take turns looking up the definitions of this week's Vocabulary words in the dictionary. Read aloud each dictionary definition. Then work together to decide what about the dictionary definition you found helpful and what was confusing. What would you do to make the definition clearer? Write your own definition.

Dramatize It

Pick a Vocabulary word. Act out the word for a partner. See if your partner can guess what word you are acting out.

Creative Connections

Choose a Vocabulary word. Think of a word that goes with it. Tell a partner why you think the two words go together.

Sensible Sentences

Write a single sentence with as many Vocabulary words as you can include. The sentence must make sense.

Telling Tales

Write a story using all of the week's Vocabulary words. If it helps, you can use any form of the word you want and you can use words more than once.

A Matter of Degree

Pick an adjective from the week's Vocabulary words, think of another word that is less intense than your word, and another that is more intense than your word.

Words Within Words

Pick a Vocabulary word and write it on a separate sheet of paper. See how many other words you can make from some or all of the letters in that word.

Rhyme Time

Pick a Vocabulary word and write words that rhyme with it. Write a sentence that uses the vocabulary word and one of the rhyming words.

Match Game

Pick three Vocabulary words and write each on a separate piece of paper. On another piece of paper write a clue for each word. Give the clues and words to a partner to match up. Check to see if he or she correctly matched the words and clues.

Word Scramble

Pick three Vocabulary words. On a separate piece of paper, write a scrambled form of each word. Ask a partner to unscramble the words.

Activities for Vocabulary Development

Antonyms and Synonyms

Pick three Vocabulary words. With a partner, brainstorm a list of as many antonyms and synonyms as you can. Afterwards, check a thesaurus to see how complete your list is.

Vocabulary Notebook

For each group of Vocabulary words you learn, keep track of which words you like best in a Vocabulary Notebook. Think about what you like best about the words you chose.

Crosswords

Build a crossword puzzle for the week's Vocabulary words. Make sure to write sensible clues that a partner can use to guess each word.

Write a Short Poem

Use as many Vocabulary words as you can in a short poem. Share your poem with a partner.

List your Favorite Words

Review this week's Vocabulary. What are some of your favorite new words that you have learned? What do you like about the words? Share your list with a partner.

Instructional Routines

Instructional Routines for Comprehension

The following routines support book discussions and modeling Think Alouds. Book discussions can be a highly valuable aspect of comprehension instruction. By engaging in rich discussions, students clarify and deepen their understanding of a text through discussion and response. Students

- increase engagement with the text and read more deeply into the text, leading to deeper comprehension.

- develop academic language by using it to express their ideas and opinions.

- draw on comprehension skills to develop higher-order thinking.

- interact with the text in order to make meaning.

The student Think-Aloud Routine can be used as part of a Book Discussion or at other times during instruction to help students think about their reading and deepen their understanding of the text.

Pages	Routine Name	Use with ...	Materials Needed
23–24	**Think-Aloud Routine**	• Reading Strategy instruction • Responding • Comprehension/Critical Thinking Questions	• Anthology
25	**Book Discussion Routine**	• Reading Strategy instruction • Responding • Supporting Comprehension questions	• Anthology • Reading Cards

Think-Aloud Routine

Purpose Use this routine and the Think Aloud prompts on page 24 to provide students with a supported approach to thinking about their reading during instruction and discussion.

TEACHER		STUDENTS
Display and read aloud one of the prompts.	*I can use the "This makes me think…" prompt during reading.*	Listen
Read aloud a portion of the text, such as a couple of interesting sentences. Model by using one of the prompts to think aloud about the text.	*When I was reading those sentences, it made me think…..*	Listen
• Tell the students that it will be their turn now. • Read another portion of the text aloud with the children.	*Take turns with a partner – each of you should talk using the prompt, "This makes me think…"*	Discuss the reading.
• Choose and read aloud more prompts. Read aloud another portion of the text. • Have students use the other prompts to continue discussing the text with their partner.	*Now use the prompts as you talk to your partner about this section of the text.*	• Listen. • Use *Think Aloud* prompts for further discussion.

Instructional Routines

Think Aloud Prompts

Prompt	What Students Might Do
This makes me think ...	• Connect prior knowledge and the text to generate inferences • Think about how a character behaved and make a prediction • Think about how the information is related to a content area such as social studies or world events
I wonder ...	• Speculate about character motives, or possible events • Ask themselves questions about the text or the author's purpose
I am surprised by ...	• Monitor original predictions and note when something different happens • Notice when characters or events take an unexpected turn • In informational text, students should identify misconceptions that students held before reading
I don't understand ...	• Identify confusing portions of the text • Challenge the actions of a character ("Why would she have done that?") • Ask questions about information that they do not understand.
This reminds me of ...	• Make connections to something similar that happened to them • Make connections to another character that is similar • Make connections to the information in relation to other knowledge, such as social studies or world events
This part must mean ...	• Restate information or talk about stories to consolidate understanding • "I think the author is saying ..."
I am picturing ...	• Visualize as they read
I didn't like it when ...	• Identify parts of a story that were unsatisfying or where they disagree with the actions of a character • Find portions of the text where the author's style or organization made the text difficult to understand

Book Discussion Routine

Organizing Book Discussions

At the beginning of the year, work with the class to establish ground rules for group discussion. These may include listening attentively, waiting for a turn to speak, and showing respect for others. Emphasize that part of being a good participant in a discussion is coming prepared. You may want to share the Tips for Discussion at right, or create your own with your class.

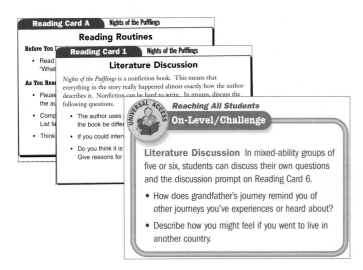

Use Reading Cards and the Literature Discussion boxes at the end of each selection for discussion questions to get you started. Initially, moderate book discussions so you can model and reinforce good discussion habits:

- respectful participation

- using text evidence in response to questions or ideas

- asking interesting questions

As students are ready, have small groups or pairs conduct independent discussion with the **Reading Cards.** Enliven discussion by forming heterogenous groups of students with varied experiences or viewpoints. You may also want to assign individual roles to discussion participants.

Tips for Book Discussion

Before Reading

☐ Be sure you have your reading notebook (or some other place) to write down your thoughts as you read.

☐ List any questions or predictions you have before you start.

During Reading

☐ Think about the story or the information.

☐ Use your reading notebook to write questions, interesting words, a quick sketch, or other reactions to the text.

Having a Discussion

☐ Come prepared—bring your notebook, your questions, and your ideas.

☐ Listen to others.

☐ Only one person should talk at a time.

☐ Try to connect what you are saying to what others have said.

☐ Stay on topic.

☐ Support your ideas by giving examples from the text.

☐ If your ideas are different from those of someone else, disagree in a respectful way.

Instructional Routines

Instructional Routines for Fluency

The Teacher's Edition of *Houghton Mifflin Reading* provides teachers with daily lessons for teaching fluency. Use the routines and program materials that follow to vary daily fluency practice, or to meet the fluency needs of individual students.

Program Materials for Fluency Practice

Anthology

Theme Paperbacks

Reader's Library

Practice Readers

Page	Routine Name
27	Choral Reading Routine
27	Partner Reading Routine
28	Echo Reading Routine
28	Repeated Reading Routine

Fluency Routines

Purpose Use these routines to provide students with opportunities to build fluency.

Choral Reading Routine

TEACHER		STUDENTS
• Read text aloud with students. • Model accuracy, appropriate rate, and expression.	*Read the text aloud with me. Adjust your reading so that we sound like one voice.*	Read text aloud with teacher.

Partner Reading Routine

TEACHER		STUDENTS
• Have two students partner read the text. • Monitor and provide corrective feedback.	*While you take turns reading the pages of this text, listen to your partner.* *Ask yourself:* *1. Is my partner reading too slowly or too quickly?* *2. Is my partner using the commas and periods?* *3. Is my partner reading the words correctly?* *4. Does my partner sound like he or she is talking?* *Help your partner by modeling when you read.*	Read a story with a partner, taking turns reading each sentence or page.
• Have students partner read the text again, switching so they read different pages this time. • Monitor and provide corrective feedback.		Read the story again, reading different pages than the first time.

Instructional Routines

Echo Reading Routine

TEACHER		STUDENTS
• Read a phrase of the text. • Model accuracy, appropriate rate, and expression.	*Listen and follow along while I read. Pay attention to the speed at which I read and how my voice changes.*	Listen to the teacher read aloud the text.
• Have students repeat the same text aloud. • Monitor as students read, and provide feedback. • Repeat the procedure with the rest of the text.	*Now you read the same text that I just read.*	Read aloud the same text that the teacher has read. Continue to listen as the teacher reads and to read the text after listening.

Repeated Reading Routine

TEACHER		STUDENTS
Select a short passage for the children to read.		
• Read the passage aloud once for comprehension. • Model accuracy, appropriate rate, and expression.	*Listen as I read the text aloud. Pay attention to the speed at which I read and how my voice changes.*	Listen as the teacher reads aloud the passage.
• Have students whisper-read the passage aloud. • Circulate and monitor children's reading. If a word is misread, read the word correctly, and have the child repeat the word before continuing.	*Now you read the passage aloud. Whisper the words so that you don't disturb others.*	Read the same passage aloud.
Have children reread the passage until the desired level of fluency is achieved.		Read the passage several more times to achieve fluency.

Instructional Routines for Corrective Feedback

Part of creating a successful classroom is ensuring that students receive all of the instruction and feedback they need in order to master academic skills. One strategy for helping students meet expectations is the use of corrective feedback.

- Corrective feedback is a point-of-use strategy that allows teachers to address students' errors as they occur. When teachers hear or see a mistake, they point it out and show students how to correct the error.

- It is important that teachers do not single out students when errors arise. Instead, they should address the mistake with the entire class. This practice will ensure that every student masters skills and meets goals.

- Using corrective feedback is an important tool as teachers monitor students' comprehension. The sooner mistakes are caught, the sooner they can be fixed.

The Teacher's Editions of *Houghton Mifflin Reading* include corrective feedback boxes that will guide you in correcting errors as students work through phonics and decoding lessons. You can also use the following routines to correct errors during additional reading tasks or small-group lessons.

Page	Routine Name	Use with . . .	Use when . . .
30	**Corrective Feedback Routine 1**	• reading tasks • Phonics/ Decoding lessons	• Students misidentify sounds for letters as they read connected text.
31	**Corrective Feedback Routine 2**	• Phonics/ Decoding lessons • Small-group Extra Support lessons	• Students need additional support with sound/spelling correspondences.

Instructional Routines

Corrective Feedback Routine 1

Purpose Use this routine to correct sound/spelling correspondence errors as students read connected text.

TEACHER		STUDENTS
Correct the error. Point to the target letter(s), letter pair, or affix. Tell students the sound. Remind them of the spelling pattern.	*Point to or underline the -ed in missed. The sound is /t/. Remember, -ed at the end of word can stand for the sound /t/ or the sound /ĕd/.*	Listen
Guide practice. Have students sound out the word with you.	*Let's sound out the word: /mĭĭĭssst/, missed*	/mĭĭĭssst/, missed
Check understanding. Have students sound out the word without assistance.	*Now you do it. What is the word?*	/mĭĭĭssst/, missed
Reinforce learning. Have students go back to the beginning of the sentence and continue reading.	*Go back to the beginning of the sentence and keep reading.*	Continue reading from the beginning of the sentence.

Corrective Feedback Routine 2

Purpose Use this routine to correct sound/spelling correspondences with students who need additional support.

TEACHER		STUDENTS
Correct the error. Tell students the correct answer.	*The word is* passage.	Listen
Model. Point out important sound/spelling correspondences, word parts, or patterns. Model how to use them to sound out the word.	*Point to or underline -age.* *Remember, the word ending -age stands for the sounds /əj/ What are the sounds for -age? /əj/*	Listen
Guide practice. Repeat the question or task, and have students respond along with you.	*What are the sounds for -age? /əj/* *What is the word? /păsssəj/, passage*	/əj/ /păsssəj/, passage
Check understanding. Have students answer the same question or complete the same task without assistance.	*Now you do it. What is the word?*	/păsssəj/, passage
Reinforce learning. Have students go back to the beginning of the sentence and continue reading.	*Go back to the beginning of the sentence and continue reading.*	Students go back to the beginning of the sentence and continue reading.

Instructional Routines

Instructional Routine for Academic Language

In order for students to learn academic language, it is important that they are given repeated opportunities to use the language. Students must not only hear academic language, but they must also apply and use the language themselves during classroom instruction, extensive independent reading, open-ended discussion, and their own writing.

In *Houghton Mifflin Reading,* you and your students will use a wide variety of academic language in the instruction surrounding each reading selection. Use the routine on the following page to guide explicit instruction in academic language. As students respond to, answer questions about, and write about the selections, make sure they use the academic language in their responses.

Lesson Type	Examples of Academic Language*	
Comprehension	author's viewpoint inferences generalizations main idea details conclusions	play narrator dialog fable moral myth
Vocabulary	antonym synonym vocabulary dictionary	definition thesaurus entry
Writing	narrative summary plot	description persuasion
Grammar	adverb conjunction preposition	subject predicate
Study Skills	glossary index	strategy research
Content-Area Reading	heritage habitat	revolution frontier

* Look for academic language terms in lesson Objective boxes.

Academic Language Routine

Purpose Use this routine to deliver academic language instruction before beginning a lesson, and to check understanding after completing the lesson.

TEACHER		STUDENTS
Write the academic language on the board.	Write *compare* and *contrast* on the board.	
• Say the words aloud, and provide students with simple explanations for each word. • Record these explanations on the board.	*Compare.* Compare *means to find out ways that things are the same.* *Contrast.* Contrast *means to find out ways that things are different.*	
Have students give their own explanations, create drawings, or act out the meanings of the words in order to reinforce meaning.	*Sam,* compare *your shoes and Lisa's shoes by telling something that is the same about them.* *Lisa,* contrast *by telling what is different about your shoes.*	Compare shoes. *When I compare my shoes and Lisa's shoes, I notice that...* Contrast shoes.
Explain to students how they can use the academic vocabulary words in the lesson.	*As we read this story, we are going to compare and contrast the characters to find out how they are alike and different.*	Compare and contrast the characters as they read.
After each lesson, have students use the academic vocabulary words to tell about what they have done. Students could also explain the meanings of the words based on what they learned in the lesson.	*What do you find out when you* compare *and* contrast *these two characters?*	When I compare *these two characters, I see that they both loved Japan and California. When I* contrast *them, I see that one moved back to Japan and the other stayed in California.*
Reinforce the academic language terms as students move through future lessons. Remind them of the language and give them opportunities to use it.	*Compare and contrast the two settings in this selection. How are they alike and different?*	Students respond using the words *compare* and *contrast*.
Include academic language terms in letters to family members. Encourage students and family members to use the academic language as they discuss homework and other take-home material.		

Instructional Routines

Instructional Routine for Timely Teacher Feedback

Timely teacher feedback is an important aspect of effectively teaching writing skills. In order for students to learn and improve their writing skills, it is necessary for teachers to provide them with continual feedback throughout the writing process. By showing students what they do well and pointing out areas where they need to improve, teachers ensure that students understand what it is expected in their writing.

As students move through the writing process in weekly lessons and in the Reading Writing Workshop, teachers should use the following steps to ensure timely teacher feedback:

- Teachers should confer with students at different points in their writing. It is important that teachers check in with students early in the writing process, such as when students are planning a longer piece or when they have half a paragraph or half a page written.

- Teachers should remind students to review the week's writing rubric. This will remind students what is expected of them.

- Teachers can keep a loose-leaf notebook with a page for each student. The notebook will allow teachers to record notes and comments on students' progress.

- Teachers can use their notes to inform instruction. If a number of students are having similar problems, teachers can give a mini-lesson to a small group or to the entire class.

Page	Routine	Use with ...	Materials Needed
35	Timely Teacher Feedback Routine	<ul><li>Daily writing lessons</li><li>Reading-Writing Workshop lessons</li><li>Students-Teacher Writing Conferences</li><li>On-Demand Writing Lessons</li></ul>	Writing Traits Rubric from the Practice Book

Timely Teacher Feedback Routine

In the back of the **Practice Book,** you can find a Writing Traits Rubric for each weekly writing assignment. These rubrics identify the writing traits that students should be focusing on in their writing. You can use the rubrics as a guide for providing students with timely teacher feedback.

Purpose Use the following routine to help students improve their writing.

Steps	Materials
Find places where the student has done a good job of incorporating a writing trait or traits. Explain what you like and why. Try to find more positive areas than problems. Ask about the strong parts: *How did you come up with this idea? Why did you choose this word/phrase?* Take notes on the student's responses.	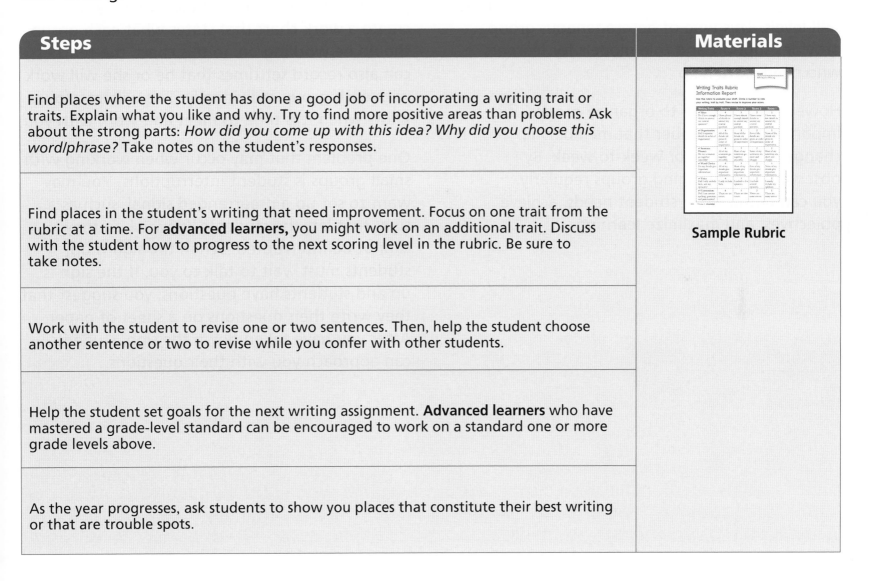 **Sample Rubric**
Find places in the student's writing that need improvement. Focus on one trait from the rubric at a time. For **advanced learners,** you might work on an additional trait. Discuss with the student how to progress to the next scoring level in the rubric. Be sure to take notes.	
Work with the student to revise one or two sentences. Then, help the student choose another sentence or two to revise while you confer with other students.	
Help the student set goals for the next writing assignment. **Advanced learners** who have mastered a grade-level standard can be encouraged to work on a standard one or more grade levels above.	
As the year progresses, ask students to show you places that constitute their best writing or that are trouble spots.	

Management Routines

Teacher-Led Instructional Groups

Forming Groups

Using flexible grouping allows teachers to organize different groups for different purposes. For example, you may decide to group students who need extra help with a particular skill. Or, you may decide to group students with different skill levels. This type of heterogeneous group provides support and role models for learners who need extra help.

However you decide to organize groups, it is important to remember that membership changes day-to-day or week-to-week. By observing and changing groups regularly, you can better meet student needs, achieve objectives, and maximize learning.

Managing Groups

In order for small groups to be effective, it is important to set up a plan for managing them. Create a schedule and a set of rules and expectations that let the students know how the groups will work. For example, you may wish to create a work chart that states what each group should be working on. In this chart, the teacher can also record set times that he or she will work with each group individually. This will let groups know when it is time to meet and work with you.

One problem that may occur when working with small groups is student interruptions. You may want to set up a prearranged signal, such as a sign, that lets the students know when they cannot be interrupted. When the sign is up, students must wait to talk to you. If the sign is up and students have questions, you suggest that they write their questions on a sheet of paper. After you have taken down the sign, students can approach you with their questions.

Ready-Made Independent Practice

While a teacher is working with a small group, it is important that the other students work independently to practice and apply critical skills. Ready-made independent practice allows students to

- practice comprehension skills and reading strategies
- increase and broaden vocabulary
- develop fluency
- use vocabulary and spelling words in meaningful practice activities
- practice writing modes and traits

Building Vocabulary Flip Chart

- Small-group activities expand vocabulary and comprehension.
- Leveled activities build background and reinforce word skills for children at all levels.
- Beautiful photographs make vocabulary accessible for English Learners.

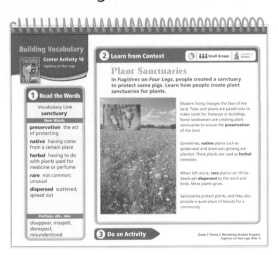

Reading in Science and Social Studies

- Flip charts and books provide independent content-area reading and activities.
- Science and Social Studies Independent Books build critical comprehension skills for nonfiction.
- Three weekly leveled activities provide critical reading skill and strategy practice appropriate for every child.

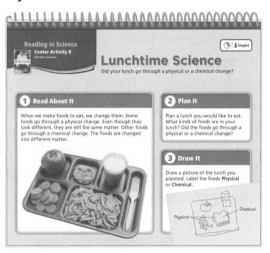

Small Group Independent Activities Kit

Weekly envelopes contain materials for each week:

- Routine, Challenge, and Activity Cards for students independence
- Spelling and Vocabulary Word flashcards for student practice
- Work Chart to group, assign, and schedule daily work

Management Routines

Using Flexible Groups

Flexible groups accommodate students' varied needs and interests.

- Homogeneous groups are organized according to need. Teachers should adjust lesson pacing and assignments for students with similar reading levels, learning styles, or abilities.

- Heterogeneous groups are organized by purpose or ability to work well together. These types of groups work well with brainstorming activities and other tasks that require a variety of opinions, approaches, and strengths. Teachers can create different ways to assign students to heterogeneous groups. For example, teachers may randomly assign different colored paper geometric shapes to students. Then, students can group themselves by matching colors and/or shapes.

Assigning Partners

When assigning partners, it is important for teachers to think about the nature of the task, as well as students' reading levels, learning styles, and abilities.

- Teachers can assign partners of similar abilities when students are practicing a skill that is new to both of them. This strategy works particularly well in an activity such as practicing spelling words.

- Teachers can assign partners of different abilities when a mentor can be helpful to a struggling learner. This works particularly well in an activity such as partner reading, where a more proficient reader can help a struggling student to read and understand more difficult texts. It also works well when matching students who share interests.

Creating Book Boxes

Book boxes are a good way for teachers to organize and store reading books for individual or group use. Teachers can make book boxes by covering old cartons or commercial magazine organizers with adhesive paper. In the book boxes, teachers can store familiar stories, books chosen by the students, and magazines or other materials that students can read independently to strengthen their reading skills.

Using Workboards

Teachers can use an Activity Workboard to show activities that students can work on if they are not meeting in a group.

- To create an Activity Workboard, teachers should think of activities that students can complete independently.

- Teachers can draw a picture or write a brief explanation that represents each activity. These pictures or explanations are compiled together to create a Workboard. Workboards can be displayed on a chalkboard or white board. They can also be displayed in the form of a pocket chart.

Sorting Papers

Students should be encouraged to take an active role in filing and storing work samples to save throughout the school year. Teachers can label a hanging file folder for each student, and hang the folders alphabetically in a cardboard carton.

- Teachers can sort portfolios, journals, and other dated samples of students' work into the folders so they will be readily available for parent conferences.

- Teachers can show students how to find their files and store their work independently. This is a hands-on way for students to practice alphabetical order and to learn to be organized.

Managing Time

Teachers should help students manage their time when working independently. Students should be reminded that it is important to know what tasks need to be done and how long they have to work, so that they can plan how to get everything done.

- For every independent activity, the teacher should talk with students about the amount of time needed to complete the activity. The time can be defined by the task, or teachers can provide a timer and give students a time limit.

- Display assigned work on the board so students know what work is required.

- Ask students to suggest activities that they can work on when they have completed assigned tasks. Display their suggestions.

Management Routines

Developing Self-Assessment

As teachers help students set goals for their own learning, students begin to see for themselves how they can improve their work.

- Teachers should encourage students to reflect on their reading and writing. Teachers can guide students with the following questions: *What did I like best about this story (my writing) and why? Why did I read (write) this? What was the best part of the activity?*

- Teachers can help students learn to evaluate their own work. The following questions can be used to guide students: *What did I do when I came to a word I did not know? Does my story make sense? Did I use describing words in my writing? Did I spell the words correctly?*

Utilizing Group Self-Assessment

Teachers can have groups that have shared a number of activities and discussions during the year meet to talk about how well the group worked together. The following questions can be used to guide the discussion:

- How well did we listen to each other?

- Did we each get a chance to say what we wanted to say?

- How well did we work together on group projects?

- Which group projects or discussions worked the best?

- Which ones did not work so well?

- What are good things to remember for future group work?

Using Peer Assessment

Students can help assess one another's work. As teachers go over an activity, they should make sure that students understand exactly what they want them to accomplish. Then, teachers can model how to give feedback.

Teachers should have students practice giving feedback to each other. At the end of the week, teachers can have pairs of students share their work and take turns helping assess each other. Teachers can use the following questions to guide students' assessments:

- What did the other student do well?

- What do you think the other student found challenging? Be specific.

- What do you think will help the other student in future activities?

Differentiated Instruction

Struggling Readers

Additional Instruction

Houghton Mifflin Reading provides thirty minutes of additional daily instruction for struggling readers. Instructional notes labeled "Extra Support" appear at point-of-use throughout the Teacher's Edition. The *Extra Support Handbook* provides daily explicit 30 minute instructional plans designed for students who are struggling. Practice Readers with small group differentiated lessons provide the application and practice that all struggling readers need to become fluent. Finally, a differentiated plan designed to help teachers organize their resources for meaningful instruction is a part of every week.

Differentiated Instruction

This differentiated instruction plan highlights weekly group and independent activities designed to meet the needs of struggling readers.

Struggling Reader Plan

Point-of-use Instruction

Extra Support boxes for struggling readers provide opportunities to reinforce a skill or concept at point-of-use.

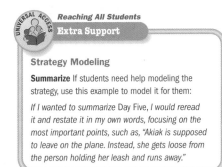

Extra Support Handbook

The *Extra Support Handbook* provides a five-day lesson plan with additional instruction for each selection in *Houghton Mifflin Reading*. The features below enable struggling readers and low performing students to achieve grade-level standards and become fluent readers.

- Preteach and reteach labels indicate when to use the lesson in relation to Core instruction.

- Skill objectives support explicit instruction.

- Literature and Skill Focus lessons support selection comprehension, writing, and grammar skills.

- Each lesson is a direct link to the literature for the week making certain that all students have a part in the community of learners.

Differentiated Instruction

Struggling Readers

Practice Readers and Lesson Plans for Struggling Readers

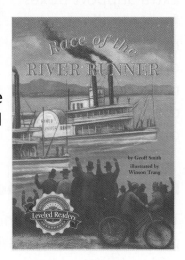

- Practice Readers build background and vocabulary.

- Comprehension skills are developed and practiced with Blackline Master support.

- Readers build fluency with critical modeling opportunities built in to the daily plan.

Tier II Vocabulary Instruction

- Weekly Vocabulary Instruction that targets Tier II words.

- Vocabulary in Context Cards that reinforce vocabulary with visual elements for struggling readers.

- Routines on each card provide a students friendly definition and learning tool.

- Vocabulary Readers reinforce Tier II words.

Flipcharts Offer Differentiated Independent Opportunities

- Children build reading comprehension while they work with Science and Social Studies content.

- Pictures, labels, and other visual elements support comprehension for all learners.

- Differentiated opportunities allow struggling readers to respond at their own level.

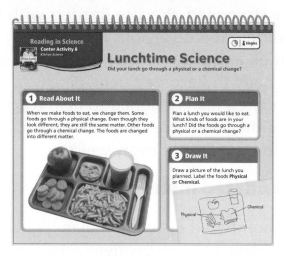

Vocabulary Development Lessons

Context Cards

Struggling Readers

Houghton Mifflin Reading Toolkit, Grade 3

The *Houghton Mifflin Reading Toolkit* provides intervention instruction for the five critical areas of reading. The 450 lessons for grades 1–3 give teachers a resource to support a huge number reading skills for those children who need an extra boost.

Portals Intensive Intervention, Grades 4–8

- An Intensive Intervention Program designed to replace the core.

- Organized in 6 levels (A-F) that correspond to the standards in grades 1–8.

- An initial Foundations Level for Portals ELD helps students with survival language as they are introduced to English.

- A thorough assessment plan helps teachers know when students need Portals and when they are ready to rejoin the Core.

Graphic Novels Provide Decodable Text

- Found in the Foundations Level, Level A and B, Graphic Novels use real-life settings to provide decodable text in a format that respects the learner and makes a real-world connection.

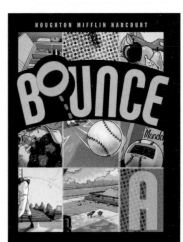

- Decodable Graphic Novels provide more than 30,000 words.

Big Words Go A Long Way!

- Semantic Maps, Games, and a personalized vocabulary journal.

Differentiated Instruction

Advanced Learners

 30 Minutes Daily

Additional Instruction

Houghton Mifflin Reading provides thirty minutes of additional daily instruction for advanced learners. Instructional notes labeled "challenge" appear at point-of-use throughout the Teacher's Edition. In addition, the *Challenge Handbook* provides daily explicit 30-minute instructional plans designed for students who are reading above grade level. Practice Readers and their accompanying small-group differentiated lessons provide the practice and application that all readers need to become fluent and to continue to grow. Vocabulary Readers designed for advanced readers extend vocabulary and build in more depth for major comprehension strategies. Finally, a differentiated plan designed to help teachers organize their resources for meaningful instruction is a part of every week.

Differentiated Instruction

This differentiated instruction plan highlights weekly group and independent activities designed to meet the needs of advanced learners.

ADVANCED LEARNERS

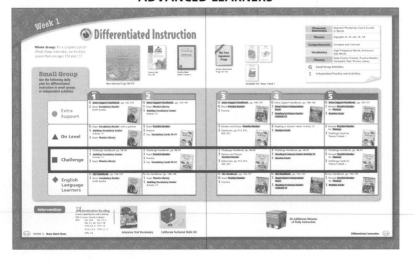

Point-of-Use Instruction

Challenge boxes for advanced learners provide opportunities to extend skills or concepts at point-of use.

Reaching All Students
Challenge

Style A writer's style is that writer's typical way of writing. Style incorporates tone, word choice, sentence length, rhythm, use of figurative language, and choice of formal or informal language, among other things. Have students look at page 64 and analyze Allen Say's style. Students should examine how he organizes his sentences, his word choices, and so on. Interested students might like to compare his writing style to his style of painting or to the haiku found in the link on pages 78–79.

Challenge Handbook

The *Challenge Handbook* delivers instructional activities that will extend advanced learners' experience with the literature and skills in *Houghton Mifflin Reading*.

The activities are presented with a five-day plan designed to engage students in higher-level thinking and exploration. The activities help prepare students to both work independently and to be an integral part of the whole group.

The activities for advanced learners are

- integrated with the content of the literature and skills in each theme;

- interdisciplinary, often including other key content areas;

- inquiry-based, helping students to learn, do research, elaborate, summarize, and synthesize.

Advanced Learners

Practice Readers and Lesson Plans for Advanced Learners

- Practice Readers extend background and vocabulary for the week's main selection

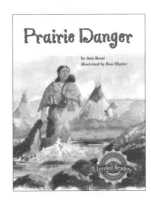

- Comprehension skills and strategies are extended to a deeper level, making higher expectations clear.

- Students continue to build fluency with models and repeated practice and student application.

Flipcharts Offer Differentiated Independent Opportunities

- Children extend reading comprehension while they work with Science and Social Studies content.

- Differentiated opportunities allow advanced learners to respond at their own level.

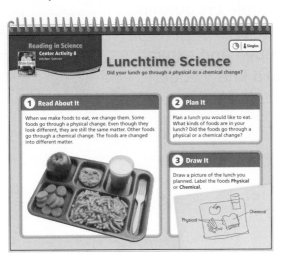

Tier II Vocabulary Instruction

- Weekly lessons develop students' Tier II vocabulary.

- Vocabulary in Context Cards reinforce vocabulary with visual elements to support all readers.

- Vocabulary Readers extend Tier II words.

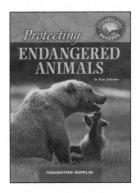
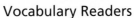

Vocabulary Readers   Context Cards

Differentiated Instruction

English Language Learners

⏱ 30 Minutes Daily

Additional Instruction

Houghton Mifflin Reading provides thirty minutes of additional daily instruction for English Language Learners. Instruction appears in point-of-use instructional notes throughout the Teacher's Edition, in the *Handbook for English Language Learners,* and in small-group lessons for Language Support Practice Readers and Vocabulary Readers.

Differentiated Instruction

The Differentiated Instruction plan highlights weekly teacher-led and independent activities designed to meet the needs of English Learners.

ENGLISH LANGUAGE LEARNERS

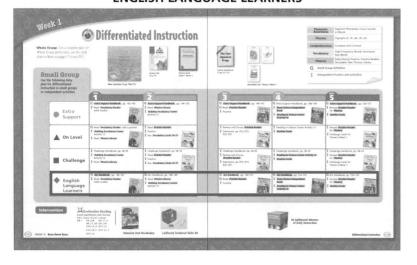

Point-of-use Instruction

Instructional boxes for English Language Learners include lesson modifications, techniques for scaffolding responses, vocabulary instruction, retelling activities, teaching tips, and question stems. Each box addresses the needs of students at different proficiency levels.

Vocabulary Readers

- High-interest nonfiction topics engage readers.

- Pictures, labels and other visual elements support comprehension.

- Multiple encounters with key vocabulary deepen and expand word knowledge.

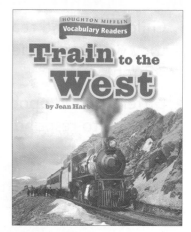

English Language Learners

Handbook for English Language Learners

This easy-to-use resource provides a five-day lesson plan with additional instruction for each selection in *Houghton Mifflin Reading*. The features below will help you support students learning English.

- Preteach and reteach labels indicate when to teach each lesson.

- Daily Language Development lessons develop vocabulary, listening, and speaking skills.

- Skill objectives and academic language support explicit instruction.

- Literature and Skill Focus lessons support selection comprehension and reinforce phonics, high-frequency words, writing, and grammar skills.

- Multi-Level Response and Practice opportunities address the needs of children at different levels of proficiency.

- Language Transfer Support notes identify areas where attempts to transfer knowledge may lead to errors in English.

- If Needed section provides additional support targeted to learners at beginning levels of proficiency.

- Other features include interactive activities, Graphic Organizers, Selection Summaries, and Blackline Masters of rhymes and chants.

Language Support Practice Readers and Lesson Plans

- Students practice and apply comprehension skills and strategies to accessible text.

- Pictures, labels and other visual elements support comprehension.

- Lesson support includes background building and vocabulary development.

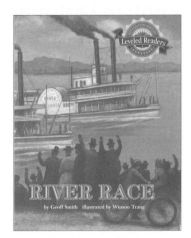

Differentiated Instruction

English Language Development System

 **60 Minutes Daily**

English Language Development System, K–6

The ELD System provides instructional materials for at least one hour per day for English Learners who need focused, systematic instruction in language and reading skills. The instructional plan includes

- formative assessment and progress monitoring
- high-quality vocabulary instruction in Tier I, II, and III vocabulary
- explicit lessons in academic language and signal words
- regularly placed peer practice to encourage students interaction and participation

The English Language Development system includes the following components:

Teacher Guide

Efficient and interactive lesson plans for 36 full weeks of instruction (minimum of one hour per day)

Practice Books

Pencil-and-paper practice with phonics, grammar, and vocabulary

Concept Readers

A full-color, content-focused little book for each week's lesson

Teacher Resource Books

Includes Scaffolded Discussion Cards for using language functions in discussions about texts and literature

English Language Development System

ELD Assessment Handbook

Progress-monitoring tests, with additional formative assessment tools to inform instruction; student model papers from students at different proficiency levels, with strategies for conferencing with young writers; listening and speaking checklists.

Transparencies

Writing models with overlays to facilitate direct instruction and modeling in California-tested writing forms and other standards-based forms

- **Word Builders (Cards and Holders)**
- **Sound/Spelling Cards**
- **Sounds of Letters CDs**
- **Audiotexts**
- **Write-on/Wipe-off Boards**
- **Picture Cards**
- **Welcome, Newcomer! Teacher Guide and Vocabulary and Concepts Posters**

A Note about Language Proficiency Levels in the Handbook for English Language Learners

Houghton Mifflin Reading uses four language proficiency levels, but generally the intermediate and early advanced levels are grouped together for a reason. Here is how the labels in *Houghton Mifflin Reading* correspond to the five proficiency levels used in California:

Houghton Mifflin Labels	California Language Proficiency Levels
Beginning/Preproduction	Beginning
Early Production/Speech Emergent	Early Intermediate
Intermediate/Advanced	Intermediate Early Advanced Advanced

We use this grouping because of the concern that the proficiency labels would have the inadvertent and unexpected effect of lowering expectations for students. We want teachers to encourage students as quickly as possible to move to the Intermediate, early advanced, and advanced levels of proficiency. To do this, once students are beginning to produce and comprehend the language, we encourage high expectations and provide maximum support for rapidly accelerating achievement so that they can participate successfully in the core curriculum. We believe that students can rapidly progress from the English Language Arts standards listed as part of English Language Development Standards at the Intermediate level, to those listed at the Early Advanced and Advanced Levels.

For example:

Once students can...

1.7 Add, delete, or change target sounds to change words (e.g. change *cow* to *how*, *pan* to *an*) (ELD **Intermediate** Reading Standard and ELA Reading Standard, Grade 1, 1.7)

They should quickly be able to...

1.8 Track (move sequentially from sound to sound) and represent changes in simple syllables and words with two and three sounds as one sound is added, substituted, omitted, or repeated (e.g. vowel-consonant, consonant-vowel, or consonant-vowel-consonant) (ELD **Early Advanced** Reading Standard and ELA Reading Standard, Grade K, 1.8)

Once students can...

1.8 Blend two to four phonemes into recognizable words (e.g. /c/a/t/ = cat; /f/l/a/t/ = flat).
(ELD **Intermediate** Reading Standards and ELA Reading Standard, Grade 1, 1.8)

They are demonstrating that they can also...

1.9 Blend vowel-consonant sounds orally to make words or syllables. (ELD **Early Advanced** Reading Standard and ELA Reading Standard, Grade K, 1.9)

We found it was more defensible to provide separate instructional strategies for students at the beginning and early intermediate stages of language proficiency, where the differences in language comprehension and production are relatively large. But because of the similarity of the standards addressed in the intermediate and early advanced, and even the advanced levels of language proficiency, we put those levels together and provided support teachers can use to quickly move students into the upper levels of proficiency.

AAVE

African American Vernacular English

Background

In recent decades, much research has been done on the language system now known as African American Vernacular English, or AAVE. Linguistics scholars such as Dr. William Labov have illustrated that, far from being a breakdown of "formal" English, African American Vernacular English is a logical language system with well-formed patterns and rules. This language system is used in African American communities throughout the country.

Because AAVE patterns occur most often in informal, everyday speech, some speakers struggle when it comes time to master sound and grammar rules of Standard English (SE), or "the language of school." For example, AAVE speakers may not hear the difference between AAVE and Standard English pronunciations of some words and therefore have trouble spelling them. Similarly, AAVE speakers may write sentences using grammatical constructions that are not conventional to Standard English.

As their teacher, you can help AAVE-speaking students observe the differences between their everyday speech and the language used in school. AAVE speakers may benefit particularly from an approach that reinforces Standard English as a means that will help them succeed in school, not a "correct" system meant to replace their everyday speech.

Using the AAVE Notes in This Book

The AAVE lessons in this book have been designed to help teachers understand common features of AAVE and to provide additional support for students acquiring Standard English.

The first section of lessons focuses on sound patterns that AAVE speakers may need practice with as they complete core reading lessons, while the second section focuses on grammatical structures. Each lesson is organized according to the Teach/Practice/Apply model used throughout this program and incorporates opportunities for students to practice speaking, reading, and writing with targeted Standard English structures. Some lessons may be useful even when not tied to core reading instruction. Keep in mind, however, that not every AAVE-speaking student will need support with every structure.

Voicing of /th/

- Speakers of African American Vernacular English use several alternate voicings of the /th/ used in Standard English. At the beginning of a word, an AAVE speaker may voice /th/ as /d/ or /t/; in the middle of a word, the AAVE speaker may use /v/; at the end of a word or syllable, the AAVE speaker may use /f/ in place of /th/.

Standard English	AAVE
this	*dis*
think	*tink*
brother	*bruvver*
birthday	*birfday*

- *Th* words present particular difficulties for AAVE speakers as they learn to spell, because these students may write words phonetically according to the AAVE pronunciations that they are accustomed to rather than according to the Standard English pronunciations.

AAVE

Teach Explain to students that the letters *th* together stand for the /th/ sound. Then write these words on the board.

> | then | through | breathe | bathroom |

Read the first word aloud, emphasizing the SE pronunciation of *th*. Have students say the SE pronunciation aloud after you. Repeat for the other words.

Practice Ask students to come to the board and circle the letters in each word above that make the sound of /th/. Spell each word aloud letter-by-letter aloud with students, then repeat the whole word again as a group (*t-h-e-n; then*).

Apply Remind students that the /th/ sound is spelled with the letters *th*. Then read the following words aloud using the SE pronunciation, telling students to listen for the sound of /th/ in each.

> | *these* | *think* | *brother* | *death* |

Have students repeat each word after you, then write it on a slip of paper. Once students have written all the words, work with them to check and correct their spellings as needed. Finally, have each student choose one of the words to use in an oral sentence.

Voicing of Final -*s* in Plurals

- Students who use AAVE sometimes omit the final *s* from plural nouns when speaking and writing. When a plural noun ends in -*ts*, some AAVE speakers may drop the /t/ sound as well or use an unstressed vowel in its place.

Standard English	AAVE
We took some *tests*.	We took some *tess* or We took some *tesses*.
They got *20 cents*.	They got 20 *cent*.

Teach Remind students that a plural noun is a word that names more than one person, place, or thing. Write the following phrases on the board and have students repeat each after you, emphasizing the /s/ or /z/ sound at the end of each plural. Point out that the -*s* ending on each noun shows that it names more than one.

> | some potatoes | 50 cents |
> | six posts | four cans of soda |

Practice Write these sentences on the board. Read them aloud and have students repeat after you, emphasizing the -*s* endings. Then have students identify each plural noun and explain what clues they used to identify it.

> She bought <u>vests</u> for the twins.
> Those <u>boys</u> are in my class.
> How many <u>dollars</u> does it cost?

Apply Write the following phrases on the board. Work with students to change each noun to its correct plural form. Then have students read the new phrases aloud, emphasizing plural endings where they appear.

Standard English	AAVE
both fist (both fists)	six carrot (six carrots)
two test (two tests)	100 coin (100 coins)

Voicing of 's in Possessive Nouns

- Speakers of Standard English (SE) may form possessives by adding 's to the end of nouns that do not end in s. They may say, for example, *Matt's bike*. However African American Vernacular English (AAVE) speakers often omit the 's. They may say *Matt bike* with the possession implied, instead of *Matt's bike*.

- AAVE speakers do include the possessive 's when no noun follows the possessor, as in *The trumpet is Leo's*. It may be helpful to point this out as you work with AAVE speakers to practice vocalizing and writing possessive nouns.

Standard English	AAVE
Mr. Smith's car	*Mr. Smith* car
the *cat's* bowl	the *cat* bowl
the *people's* coats	the *people* coats

Teach Remind students that in Standard English, they add 's to the end of most singular nouns to show ownership or possession. They also add 's to plural nouns that do not end in s.

Write the examples below on the board. Read each aloud, emphasizing the 's ending to model its vocalization. Have students repeat after you, following your model. Point out that students must pronounce the 's at the end of each possessive noun so that listeners will clearly understand that the word shows ownership.

> Mary's: This is Mary's hat.
> Tisha's: Those boots are Tisha's.
> children's: Here is the children's room.

Practice Write these sentence pairs on the board and read them aloud with students, emphasizing the 's ending of each possessive noun. Then have partners take turns reading the sentences aloud to each other, with extra attention to the 's ending.

> The papers are Leon's. They are Leon's papers.
> That sandwich is Michelle's. It is Michelle's sandwich.
> The gloves are the men's. They are the men's gloves.

Apply Have each student write a sentence using a possessive noun to describe something that belongs to someone. Then ask students to read their sentences to a partner. Remind them to vocalize the 's ending of each possessive noun.

AAVE

Voicing of /v/ and /z/

- AAVE speakers sometimes replace /v/ and /z/ sounds in the middles of words with /b/ or /d/ sounds. This presents particular challenges for AAVE speakers as they learn to spell words with medial /v/ and /z/.

Standard English	AAVE
seven kids	*seben* kids
She *isn't* here.	She *idn't* here.

Teach Explain to students that in Standard English, the letter *v* makes the sound /v/. Also explain that the letter *s* sometimes makes the sound /z/ in Standard English, especially when appearing in the middle of a word. Then write these words on the board.

> seven   shovel   isn't   hasn't

Read each word aloud, emphasizing the SE pronunciation of the medial /v/ or /z/. Have students say each SE pronunciation aloud after you.

Practice Without erasing the above words, write these additional words on the board and read them aloud. Spell each word letter-by-letter with students, then say the whole word again as a group.

> wasn't   eleven   heaven   doesn't

Have students tell which words include the /v/ sound and which include the /z/ sound.

Apply Have each student choose one of the eight words at left to use in a written sentence. Students can then read their written sentences aloud to partners using Standard English pronunciations of /v/ and /z/.

Voicing of /r/

- There are several situations in which AAVE speakers may struggle with the pronunciation of /r/ as used in Standard English. See the examples below.

Standard English	AAVE
four	*fo'*
Florida	*Flo' ida or Flo' da*
better	*bettuh*
throw	*th'ow*

- The first three examples demonstrate the omission of /r/ from *r*-controlled vowel sounds as they would be used in Standard English. AAVE speakers may omit this /r/ when part of an *r*-controlled vowel sound in the middle or end of a word. Sometimes, as in the case of *fo'* and *Flo'ida*, the speaker will omit the /r/ sound completely; other times, as in the case of *bettuh*, the speaker may replace the entire *r*-controlled vowel sound with *-uh*.

- In the fourth example, the /r/ sound has been omitted from an initial consonant cluster that contains the letter *r*. AAVE speakers may need particular support when learning to spell words that fit this pattern, as they may not hear a difference between AAVE and Standard English pronunciations.

Teach Point out to students that the letter *r* in words is voiced in Standard English as /rrrr/. Then write the following words on the board and have students repeat after you, emphasizing the /r/ sound in each.

bigger	store	brought
interested	farther	four

Practice Spell each of the words above aloud with students, then repeat each complete word. Have students come to the board and circle the letter or letters in each that make the /r/ sound.

Apply Write the following words on the board and have students read each aloud, using the Standard English pronunciation of /r/.

through	door	snore
North Carolina	harder	

Have each student use one of the words in a written sentence and share that sentence orally with a partner.

Voicing of /l/

The Standard English sound of /l/ is often omitted from AAVE speech or pronounced almost as a vowel, particularly when it appears at the end of a word or directly before or after a vowel. Not surprisingly, then, AAVE speakers may not vocalize the '*ll* found in contractions of the verb *will*. This can present spelling challenges for AAVE speakers as well as difficulty in expressing the future tense with contractions.

Standard English	AAVE
people	*peopuh*
help	*he'p*
toll	*toah*
He'll be here	*He* be here

Teach Explain to students that in Standard English, the letter *l* makes the sound /l/. Then write these words on the board.

people	help	toll	he'll

Read each word aloud, emphasizing the SE pronunciation of /l/ when it appears. Have students say each SE pronunciation aloud after you. Point out that in the example *he'll*, the /l/ sound actually stands for the word *will*.

Practice Write the following sentences on the board and read them aloud for students. Have students identify the word in each that includes the /l/ sound, explain how they know, then practice saying these /l/ words aloud with Standard English pronunciation.

I have a little kitten. (little)
Is there any more milk? (milk)
It's cool. (cool)
It'll be 10:00. (It'll)

Point out that without the /l/ sound in *It'll* in the last sentence, the meaning of the sentence would change to tell about the time now, not what time it *will* be in the future.

Apply Read the following list of words and accompanying sentences aloud using Standard English pronunciation. Have students repeat each sentence after you and write the underlined words on a scrap of paper. When finished, work with students to check their spellings.

> belt: My belt is brown.
>
> coal: The stove burns coal.
>
> couple: I bought a couple of books.
>
> they'll: They'll be here soon.

Voicing of /ĭ/ and /ĕ/ Before /m/ and /n/

- Students who speak AAVE may not differentiate between the Standard English vowel sounds /ĭ/ and /ĕ/, particularly when one of these vowels appears before /m/ or /n/ in a word. As a result, words such as *pin* and *pen* may be pronounced and sound the same to AAVE speakers.

- Some students may also pronounce the Standard English /ĭ/ as /ă/ when it appears in words that end with –ing or –ink.

Standard English	AAVE
pen, pin	*pin, pen*
him	*hem*
think	*thank*
sing	*sang*

Teach Read the following word pairs aloud. Explain that your first pronunciation is one that people may use when speaking outside of school, while your second pronunciation is the Standard English pronunciation used in school. Have students describe the difference they hear in each pair.

> hem, him   lank, link   min, men   thang, thing

Point out that in all cases, the difference is related to the vowel sound /ĭ/ as in *pin* or /ĕ/ as in *pen*.

Practice Write each of the following words on the board and have students practice reading them aloud with Standard English pronunciation, focusing on /ĕ/ and /ĭ/ sounds.

> send   wing   tin   sink   dent

Apply Write the following sentences on the board and read them aloud. Have students identify the words that have been misspelled and discuss how the misspelling might confuse a reader as to the sentence's meaning. Have students correct the misspelled words, read them aloud, and then read the corrected sentences as a group.

> I thank you are funny. (think)
>
> She has tin pincils. (ten, pencils)
>
> What a pretty gold rang. (ring)

Voicing of Consonant Clusters

- In Standard English as well as other forms speakers may occasionally drop the second consonant in a two-consonant cluster. This is particularly common when the cluster appears at the end of a word and is followed by another word that begins with a consonant. AAVE speakers do this much more frequently, however.

- AAVE speakers may also drop the second consonant in a cluster when it appears at the very end of a sentence.

- Some AAVE speakers vocalize consonant blends such as –mp, -nt, -nk, -lp, -lt, and –lk with a weakened first consonant.

- AAVE speakers often also eliminate the sound of /t/ when part of the blend –ts, particularly in contractions.

Standard English	AAVE
Find it!	*Fine* it!
We hit a *bump*.	We hit a *bu'p*.
It's time for dinner.	*I's* time for dinner.

Teach Read the following word pairs aloud. Explain that your first pronunciation is one that people may use when speaking outside of school, while your second pronunciation is the Standard English pronunciation used in school. Have students describe the difference they hear in each pair.

> accep, accept   wil', wild   fis', fist
>
> he'p, help   lo's, lots

Point out that in each case, the difference is in the voicing of a consonant sound.

Practice Write each of the following words on the board and have students practice reading them aloud with Standard English pronunciation, focusing on distinguishing and voicing the distinct sounds in each blend.

> what's   respect   cold
>
> mist   that's   camp

Apply Read the following words aloud, emphasizing the consonant blend in each, and have students repeat after you. Have students write each word on a scrap of paper.

> *it's   fold   desk   hunt   trust*

Work with students to check their spellings. Then have each student choose one of the words to incorporate into an oral sentence, using the Standard English pronunciation.

AAVE

Transposition of Consonants

One distinctive feature of AAVE speech is the occasional transposition of adjacent consonants in consonant blends. See the examples below.

Standard English	AAVE
ask	aks
asking	aksing
wasp	waps

Teach Write the following words on the board.

> grasp   asked   risk   wasp   task

Sound each word out with students as you run your finger under it letter by letter, emphasizing the distinction and placement of consonant sounds in each consonant blend.

Practice Remind students that a consonant is any letter other than *a, e, i, o, u,* or *y.* Have students come to the board and circle all the places in the words listed above where two consonants appear next to one another. Then have students read the words aloud again, sounding them out slowly.

Apply Have each student write a sentence using one of the words above. Students can then read their sentences orally to partners, using Standard English pronunciations.

Voicing of Consonants in Contractions

As discussed elsewhere, many AAVE speakers struggle with the Standard English voicing of consonant clusters. This has particular implications as AAVE speakers learn to work with contractions since the omission of consonant sounds from contracted forms can lead to spelling difficulties and, in some cases, make it difficult for listeners to distinguish negative forms from positive forms. AAVE speakers are most likely to omit the sound of /t/ from contractions.

Standard English	AAVE
It's time to go.	*I's* time to go.
Don't do that.	*Don'* do that.

Teach Write the following contractions on the board and read them aloud running your finger under each letter by letter. Emphasize the sound of /t/. Have students repeat after you.

> it's   don't   can't   isn't   won't

Practice Remind students that a contraction is two words put together, with one or more letters replaced by an apostrophe. Also remind them that many contractions are formed with the word *not.* In these contractions, not is spelled *n't* and pronounced in Standard English as *nt.* Then write the following sentences on the board.

> I <u>can</u> go to school today. (can't)
>
> <u>Don</u> forget your book. (Don't)
>
> <u>Is</u> hot out. (It's)
>
> He <u>hasn</u> got it. (hasn't)

Explain to students that the underlined words are all misspelled contractions. Work with students to correct these misspellings and read the corrected sentences aloud. Ask them to discuss how each misspelling might confuse a reader.

Apply Ask students the following questions and have them respond to each in the negative, using the appropriate contraction and voicing its ending. Model the correct answer format and Standard English pronunciation as needed. For example: *Is he coming? No, he isn't.*

> Are they coming? (No, they aren't.)
> Can you do it? (No, I can't.)
> Did she play with you? (No, she didn't.)
> Have you seen it? (No, I haven't.)

Voicing of Inflected *–ed* Endings

- In keeping with the devoicing of other final consonant sounds, AAVE speakers often drop inflected *–ed* endings from words. This can create tense confusion, as the *–ed* ending is sometimes the only marker of past tense in a sentence.

- Additionally, AAVE speakers sometimes double the inflected *–ed* ending on past tense verbs.

Standard English	AAVE
I walked yesterday.	*I walk yesterday.*
We picked the fruit.	*We pickted the fruit.*

Teach Read the following words aloud, emphasizing the final *–ed* endings and running your finger under each letter by letter as you go. Have students repeat after you.

> picked   walked   rushed   liked   approved

Explain to students that the *–ed* ending on each word lets them know that the action took place in the past. Have them discuss how the meaning might change if the *–ed* ending was dropped from these words in speaking or writing.

Practice Write these sentences on the board and read them aloud, emphasizing the *–ed* endings where they appear. Have students raise their hands for each sentence that tells about something that happened in the past and explain how they know.

> He wanted a bicycle. (past tense: wanted)
> The cat scratched the chair. (past tense: scratched)
> Everyone likes Lisa.
> She cooked dinner. (past tense: cooked)
> I clean the floor.
> Sammy washed the dishes. (past tense: washed)

Have students read the past tense sentences aloud, emphasizing the sound of final *–ed* where it appears.

AAVE

Apply Have each student write a sentence about something he or she did yesterday, using an *–ed* verb. Students can then share their finished sentences with partners, focusing on the Standard English voicing of *–ed*.

Initial /d/ and /g/ Deletion

- Students who use AAVE may omit /d/ or /g/ sounds from the beginnings of words. This occurs most frequently with certain verbs such as *don't*, *going to*, and sometimes *didn't*.

Standard English	AAVE
I *don't* think so.	I *'on'* know.
I *didn't* see it.	I *'idn't* see it.
It's *going to* rain.	I's *'onna* rain.

Teach Write the following words on the board and have students repeat each after you, emphasizing the /d/ or /g/ sound at the beginning of each. Explain to students that they should vocalize these sounds clearly. You may also explain that the word *gonna*, which means *going to*, is not used in Standard English.

> don't   didn't   going to

Practice Write the following sentences on the board and have students repeat each after you, emphasizing the /d/ or /g/ sound at the beginning of each underlined word or phrase.

> I <u>don't</u> know. They <u>don't</u> like it.
> I'm <u>going to</u> go. He's <u>going to</u> call me.
> They <u>didn't</u> show up.

Apply Have each student write a sentence using *don't* or *going to*. Each student can then share his or her sentence with the group orally, using Standard English pronunciations.

Voicing of *g* in *–ing* Endings

Some AAVE speakers may vocalize inflected *–ing* endings of words as /n/. This occurs most frequently with gerunds.

Standard English	AAVE
walking	*walkin'*
thinking	*thinkin'*

Teach Explain to students that the letters *–ng* together are pronounced in Standard English as /ng/, like *bring*. Then write these words on the board.

> looking   running   wondering   eating

Read the first word aloud, emphasizing the SE pronunciation of *ng*. Have students say the SE pronunciation aloud after you. Repeat for the other words.

Practice Ask students to come to the board and circle the letters in each word above that make the sound of /ng/. Spell each word aloud letter-by-letter with students, then repeat the whole word again as a group (*l-o-o-k-i-n-g; looking*).

Apply Remind students that the /ng/ sound is spelled with the letters ng and is often used as part of an *–ing* ending. Then read these words aloud using the SE pronunciation, telling students to listen for the sound of /ng/ in each.

> walking   watching   hoping   picking

Have students repeat each word after you, then write it on a slip of paper. Once students have written all the words, work with them to check and correct their spellings as needed. Finally, have each student choose one of the words to use in an oral sentence.

Deletion of Unstressed Syllables

In some situations, AAVE speakers may drop unstressed syllables from words, particularly initial and medial syllables. See the examples below.

Standard English	AAVE
afraid	'fraid
secretary	sec't'ry

Teach Explain to students that if they clearly vocalize all the syllables in words when they speak, they may find it easier to spell them. Then write the following words on the board and read them aloud, carefully segmenting the syllables as you go. Have students repeat each word after you.

> express   secretary   especially   allow

Practice Write the following sentences on the board read them aloud.

> I'm fraid of snakes. (afraid)
> It's bout time for bed. (about)
> The movie was intrsting. (interesting)

Have students identify the words that have been misspelled, pointing out that each is missing letters for one or more syllable. Have students correct the misspelled words, read them aloud, and then read the corrected sentences as a group.

Apply Have each student share an oral sentence using one of the featured words from the Teach and Practice sections above, focusing on Standard English pronunciations.

Syllable Emphasis

Some AAVE speakers may use non-standard syllable emphasis, placing stress on the first syllable of a word whereas Standard English would place stress on the second syllable.

Standard English	AAVE
po-LICE	PO-lice
re-PEAT	RE-peat

Teach Write the following words on the board, including underlines. Explain to students that in any word with more than one syllable (or word part), one syllable is vocalized more forcefully than the others. Read the examples below aloud and have students repeat after you, imitating your syllable emphasis.

> ho<u>tel</u>   re<u>move</u>   po<u>lice</u>   de<u>feat</u>

Practice Now write these additional words on the board. Read each aloud using Standard English emphasis, have students repeat after you, and then have them identify the letters that are stressed.

> re<u>peat</u>   mo<u>tel</u>   des<u>troy</u>   re<u>member</u>

Apply Read the following sentences aloud, pronouncing the underlined words as indicated. Have students raise their hands when you use non-standard syllable emphasis in a word.

> *I got to my <u>ho-TEL</u> late last night. The next thing I <u>RE-call</u> (re-CALL) is hearing a loud noise. I wondered if I should call the <u>PO-lice</u> (po-LICE). Then the <u>HO-tel</u> (ho-TEL) owner came by. She said that a bird had flown through the front door and knocked some things over. She had already <u>re-MOVED</u> the bird. I was <u>RE-lieved</u> (re-LIEVED).*

Have students tell how these word are pronounced with Standard English emphasis.

Subject-Verb Agreement

- Speakers of African American Vernacular English often struggle with Standard English subject-verb agreement. With present-tense regular verbs, for example, AAVE speakers omit the –*s* from the end of third-person singular verbs, saying *he walk* instead of the Standard English *he walks*.

- Similarly, AAVE speakers may use first-person singular forms in place of third-person singular forms for certain irregular verbs, particularly *to do* and *to have*. An AAVE speaker might say *he do it* whereas the Standard English would be *he does it*.

- AAVE speakers also sometimes use the first person singular verb form of *to be (was)* with plurals when speaking in the past tense, saying for example *they was here* rather than *they were here*.

Standard English	AAVE
She *sits* alone.	She *sit* alone.
He *does* a good job.	He *do* a good job.
Mark *has* two dogs.	Mark *have* two dogs.
We *were* talking.	We *was* talking.

Teach Explain to students that in Standard English, many verbs use one form for *I*, *you*, *they*, and *we* and a different form for *he*, *she*, and *it*. Write the following examples on the board to illustrate this point.

I <u>sit</u>	I <u>do</u>
he/she/it <u>sits</u>	he/she/it <u>does</u>
you/we/they <u>sit</u>	you/we/they <u>do</u>
I <u>have</u>	I <u>was</u>
he/she/it <u>has</u>	he/she/it <u>was</u>
you/we/they <u>have</u>	you/we/they <u>were</u>

Read each conjugation aloud and have students repeat after you. Ask them to note the differences they see and hear within each conjugation, particularly the sound of /s/ or /z/ at the ends of forms that agree with *he*, *she*, or *it*.

Practice Write the following sentences on the board and have students change each verb form to reflect Standard English subject-verb agreement. Read the new sentences aloud together.

> It cost a dollar. (It costs a dollar.)
>
> It do not make sense. (It does not make sense.)
>
> You was wrong. (You were wrong.)
>
> Tim have a brother. (Tim has a brother.)

Apply Have each student dictate a sentence for a partner, making sure to use Standard English subject-verb agreement. Work with students to check and correct their sentences for agreement as needed.

Construction of Past Tense

When speaking and writing in the past tense, students who use AAVE may use non-standard past-tense constructions. In particular, AAVE speakers may double the inflected *–ed* endings of past tense regular verbs or add *–ed* to irregular forms that are already in the past tense.

Standard English	AAVE
I *liked* the movie.	I *likeded the movie.*
She put *her toys away.*	She putted *her toys away.*

Teach Explain to students that they can add –ed to the end of the infinitive forms of most verbs to show that an action took place in the past. In Standard English, it is not necessary to add the *–ed* more than once. Additionally, some verbs do not follow the *-ed* rule and have special past tense forms that do not require the addition of *–ed* at all. Use the following examples to illustrate, reading them aloud and having students repeat after you.

> I looked   she wrote   they wished   you sang

Practice Write the following sentence pairs on the board, read them aloud, and have students identify which sentence in each pair follows the Standard English rules.

> I picked it. I pickted it.
>
> She putted her hat on. She put her hat on.
>
> Mark likeded him. Mark liked him.
>
> He knew the answer. He knowed the answer.

Have students read the Standard English sentences aloud.

Apply Have each student share an oral sentence that tells about a fun experience he or she had recently. Remind students to use the correct past tense forms of verbs in their sentences. Ask the group to write down any past tense verbs they hear.

Use of *be* for *am/is/are/will be*

- Speakers of AAVE sometimes use *be* universally in place of Standard English past-tense forms of *to be*, saying for example *I be going* instead of *I am going*.

- AAVE speakers sometimes also use *be* in place of *will* or *will be* when expressing the future tense, as in *I be leaving* instead of *I will be leaving*. This substitution may create tense confusion, as *will* is sometimes the only word in a sentence indicating that an action will take place in the future.

Standard English	AAVE
You *are* walking to school today.	You *be* walking to school today.
I *will be* walking tomorrow.	I *be* walking tomorrow.
They *will be going* or They *will go*.	They *be* going.

AAVE

Teach Explain to students that the verb *be* is usually used in Standard English as part of a verb phrase, not on its own. Demonstrate this point by writing the following sentences on the board, reading them aloud, and telling students that only the second sentence in each pair uses Standard English verb forms.

> We *be* tired. We *are* tired.
>
> They *be eating* at 6:00. They *will be eating* at 6:00.
>
> I *be studying* tonight. I *will be studying* tonight.

Have students notice the differences between the sentences in each pair and then read the Standard English sentences aloud after you.

Practice Write these sentences on the board. Have students work together to complete each with the Standard English form of *to be*, using sentence context to decide on correct subject-verb agreement and tense. Read the completed sentences aloud as a group.

> Nora _____ happy today. (is)
>
> My neighbor's dogs _____ barking right now. (are)
>
> She _____ here later. (Possible responses: will be, will come)
>
> I _____ late if the bus doesn't come. (will be)

Apply Have each student share or write a sentence about something that he or she is doing now or will do in the future. Remind students to use Standard English forms of verbs in their sentences.

Use of *been* for *has* or *have been*

In Standard English, the word *been* is used as part of verb phrases *has been* or *have been*. AAVE speakers sometimes use *been* alone in these situations, dropping *has* or *have*.

Standard English	AAVE
She *has been* sick.	She been *sick*.
I *have been* trying.	I been *trying*.

Teach Explain to students that in Standard English, the word *been* is commonly used as part of the verb phrases *has been* or *have been*, not by itself. To illustrate this point, write the following sentences on the board, read them aloud with emphasis on the underlined verb phrases, and have students repeat after you.

> He <u>has been</u> worried.
>
> You <u>have been</u> a big help.
>
> The roof <u>has been</u> fixed.
>
> The Smiths <u>have been</u> our neighbors for years.

Practice Write the following sentences on the board. Have students work together to complete each with *has been* or *have been*, using sentence context to decide on correct subject-verb agreement. Read the completed sentences aloud as a group.

> Tina _____ _____ in school. (has been)
>
> Everyone _____ _____ busy. (has been)
>
> We _____ _____ ready for an hour. (have been)
>
> My friend and I _____ _____ to New York. (have been)

Apply Have each student complete the sentence frame: *I have been _____ for a long time.* Students can then share their sentences with the group orally or by writing them on the board.

Insertion of *done* within verbs

AAVE speakers sometimes use *done* in past-tense verb phrases to emphasize that an action has been completed. Sometimes the words in the verb phrase are left intact when *done* is added, while in other cases *done* replaces a word.

Standard English	AAVE
He *finished* practicing.	He *done finished* practicing.
Wade *has gone* or Wade *went*.	Wade *done gone*.

Teach Explain to students that in Standard English, it is not usually necessary to add *done* to a sentence to show that an action has been completed. Write the following sentence pairs on the board and read them aloud for students, emphasizing that the second sentence in each pair has been written in Standard English.

> She <u>done</u> <u>did</u> it. She <u>did</u> it.
> The kids <u>done finished</u>. The kids <u>finished</u>.
> Our friends <u>done left</u>. Our friends <u>left</u>.

Read the Standard English sentences aloud and have students repeat after you.

Practice Now write the following sentences on the board and read them aloud for students. Work with the group to identify places where the word *done* can be deleted, noting that in some places it must be replaced with the word *have* or *has*.

> I <u>done</u> washed the dishes already.
> Someone <u>done</u> wrecked our garden.
> The squirrels <u>done gone</u>. (replace *done* with *have*)

Apply Have each student create an oral or written sentence describing something he or she finished recently, such as a book or school project. Remind students that it is not necessary to use the word *done* to express that the action has been completed.

Use of Past Participle as Past Tense

Some AAVE speakers may substitute the past participle form of a verb for its past tense form in speaking or writing. See the examples below.

Standard English	AAVE
She *saw* him yesterday.	She *seen* him yesterday.
We *did* it already.	We *done* it already.

AAVE

Teach Explain that, when telling about something that happened in the past, it is important to use the correct past tense verb form. To illustrate, write the following sentence pairs on the board and read them aloud.

> She <u>seen</u> him yesterday. She <u>saw</u> him yesterday.
>
> We <u>done</u> it already. We <u>did</u> it already.

Explain to students that the verb forms *seen* and *done* do not usually appear by themselves in Standard English, as they are shown in the first sentence in each pair. Point out that the second sentence in each pair means the same thing but is written in Standard English. Have students repeat the Standard English sentences after you.

Practice Write these additional sentences on the board and work with students to complete them using the SE past tense form of the verb in parentheses.

> She _____ lions at the zoo. (to see) (saw)
>
> The rain _____ away. (to go) (went)
>
> The boys _____ the whole thing by themselves. (to do) (did)

Apply Have each student create an oral or written sentence using the standard past tense form of *to see*, *to go*, or *to do*. Have students share their sentences with partners.

Use of Verb Stem as Past Tense

AAVE speakers may sometimes substitute verb stems for past tense forms in speaking or writing. See the examples below.

Standard English	AAVE
He *came* down last night.	He *come* down last night.
We *rode* the bus this morning.	We *ride* the bus this morning.

Teach Explain to students that, when telling about something that happened in the past, it is useful to use Standard English past tense verb forms. To illustrate, write the following sentence pairs on the board and read them aloud.

> He <u>come</u> down last night. He <u>came</u> down last night.
>
> We <u>rode</u> the bus this morning. We <u>ride</u> the bus this morning.

Have students note the difference between the underlined verbs in each pair. Explain that the second sentence in each pair is written in Standard English using the past tense form of the underlined verb. Have students repeat the Standard English sentences after you.

Practice Write these additional sentences on the board and work with students to complete them using the SE past-tense form of the verb in parentheses. Read the completed sentences aloud.

> Michael _____ the train all night. (to ride) (rode)
>
> They _____ one book each day for a week. (to read) (read)
>
> Water _____ rushing down the hill. (to come) (came)

Apply Have each student create an oral or written sentence using the standard past tense form of *to ride*, *to read*, or *to come*. Have students share their sentences with partners.

Deletion of *to be* Verbs

AAVE speakers sometimes omit verb forms from present tense statements, saying for example *He here* instead of the Standard English *He is here*. This tendency extends to contractions based on nouns and pronouns as well, from which an AAVE speaker may eliminate the contracted verb and say the noun or pronoun only.

Standard English	AAVE
We are happy.	*We* happy.
He's coming.	*He* coming.

Teach Explain to students that they should always clearly vocalize verbs when speaking, even when the verb is part of a contraction. Then write the following sentences on the board and read them aloud, emphasizing the *to be* verb or contraction in each. Have students repeat after you.

> They <u>are</u> happy.
>
> He<u>'s</u> coming to the party.
>
> You <u>are</u> here.
>
> We<u>'re</u> tired.

Practice Write the following sentences on the board and tell students that each is missing its verb.

> He my older brother. (He <u>is</u> my older brother.)
>
> We all wet. (We <u>are</u> all wet.)
>
> They funny. (They<u>'re</u> funny.)
>
> She cooking already. (She<u>'s</u> cooking already.)

Work with students to add the missing *to be* verb to each sentence, using contractions in the third and fourth sentences. Read the sentences aloud again, having students repeat after you.

Apply Have each student create a written or oral sentence to describe a friend or friends. Have students use present tense *to be* verbs in their sentences.

AAVE

Word Order with Questions

- Speakers of AAVE sometimes form questions without inverting the subject and auxiliary verb as is done customarily in Standard English.
- AAVE often handles embedded questions differently than Standard English as well. When a question is embedded in a statement and, in Standard English, would include the word *if* or *whether*, an AAVE speaker may omit these words and instead invert the subject and auxiliary verb as if asking the question directly.

Standard English	AAVE
Why *is she* mad?	Why *she is* mad?
He asked *if we could* go.	He asked *could we* go.
I need to know *whether they are* coming.	I need to know *are they* coming.

Teach Explain that the order of words in questions is different than the order of words in statements. In a statement, the subject of the sentence (who or what is doing something) usually comes before the verb. In a question, the verb or part of the verb usually comes first. Write these examples on the board and have students repeat after you.

> I am going. Are you going?
>
> She can cook. Can you cook?

Next, explain that some sentences include questions without asking the questions directly. These sentences usually include the words *if* or *whether*. In these sentences, the word order does not change as it would in a question. Write these examples on the board, read them aloud, and have students repeat after you. Point out that each sentence ends with a period.

> I asked if you are going.
>
> He asked whether she can cook.

Practice Write the following on the board. Work with students to change the word order in each to reflect Standard English usage, adding *if* or *whether* when necessary. Read the new sentences aloud and have students repeat after you.

> How you are feeling? (How are you feeling?)
>
> I wonder will she come. (I wonder whether she will come.)
>
> When she is coming? (When is she coming?)
>
> We don't know can they help. (We don't know if they can help.)

Apply Have each student ask a partner a question that begins with *can*, using the Standard English word order. Have the partner restate the question using *if* or *whether*. Model as needed. For example: *Can you sing? You asked if I can sing.*

Use of *here go* for *here is*

AAVE speakers sometimes use the phrase *here go* in place of the Standard English *here is*. See the examples below.

Standard English	AAVE
Here is my drawing.	*Here go* my drawing.
Here are the bikes.	*Here go* the bikes.

Teach Explain to students that when they are presenting something or announcing it with the word *here*, Standard English uses *to be* verbs (typically *is* or *are*). Write the following examples on the board, read them aloud, and have students repeat after you.

> Here is my house.   Here are my friends.
>
> Here is my painting.

Practice Write the following on the board. Work with students to change the underlined verb in each sentence to reflect Standard English usage. Remind them to use the singular *is* with nouns that name one person, place, or thing and the plural *are* with nouns that name more than one. Read the new sentences aloud and have students repeat after you.

> Here go my shoes. (Here are my shoes.)
>
> Here go the bus. (Here is the bus.)
>
> Here go our classroom. (Here is our classroom.)
>
> Here go the librarian. (Here is the librarian.)

Apply Have each student create a written or oral statement about something found in your classroom, beginning with *Here is* or *Here are*. Have students share their work with the group.

Existential Constructions

In Standard English, the phrases *there is* or *there are* are customarily used to state the existence of something, as in *There are three apples on the table*. African American Vernacular English, however, often uses *it is* or *it's* in place of both *there is* and *there are*. *It's* is often voiced as *i's* in keeping with the dropping of the /t/ sound from the contracted form.

Standard English	AAVE
There is a man at the door.	*It's* a man at the door or *I's* a man at the door.
There are a lot of birthdays today.	*I's* a lot of birthdays today.

AAVE

Teach Explain to students that in Standard English, many statements begin with *there is* or *there are*. Write the following examples on the board, read them aloud, and have students repeat after you.

> There is an alarm ringing.
>
> There are three apples left.
>
> There is nothing you can do about it.
>
> There are a lot of birds singing.

Practice Write the following on the board. Work with students to change the underlined phrase in each to reflect Standard English usage. Remind students to use the singular *is* with nouns that name one person, place, or thing and the plural *are* with nouns that name more than one. Read the new sentences aloud and have students repeat after you.

> It's no sandwiches left. (There are no sandwiches left.)
>
> It's two sets of twins in my class. (There are two sets of twins in my class.)
>
> It's someone at the door. (There is someone at the door.)
>
> It's a loud noise outside. (There is a loud noise outside.)

Apply Have each student create a written or oral statement describing a prominent feature of your town or city, beginning each with *There is* or *There are*. Have students share their work with the group.

Possessive Pronouns

- AAVE speakers may use several non-standard ways of expressing possession. Some AAVE speakers may use *–s* at the end of the possessive pronoun *mine*, for example, instead saying *mines*.

- The possessive pronoun *whose* is not commonly used in AAVE; AAVE speakers may use *who* in its place, saying *Who book is this?* instead of the Standard English *Whose book is this?*

- The word *y'all* is often used in AAVE in place of the Standard English *your*, while *they* is often used in place of *their*.

Standard English	AAVE
That coat is *mine*.	That coat is *mines*.
I don't know *whose* hat this is.	I don't know *who* hat this is.
It's *your* ball.	It's *y'all* ball.
Where is *their* house?	Where is *they* house?

Teach Explain to students that a possessive pronoun is a pronoun that shows ownership. Write the following phrases on the board and read them aloud for students, emphasizing the underlined possessive pronouns. Have students repeat after you.

> The book is mine.   It's your house
>
> Whose pen is this?   It's their turn.

Practice Write these sentences on the board and read them aloud. Explain that in each case, the underlined word is a non-standard possessive pronoun. Work with students to replace each underlined word with the Standard English possessive (*mine, your, their,* or *whose*), then have students read the new sentences aloud.

> That's y'all fault. (That's your fault.)
>
> The red gloves are mines. (The red gloves are mine.)
>
> We don't know who book it is. (We don't know whose book it is.)
>
> Give them they tickets. (Give them their tickets.)

Apply Have each student use *your, mine, their,* or *whose* in an oral or written sentence. Students can share their sentences with partners.

Use of Object Pronouns for Reflexive Pronouns

AAVE speakers may use object pronouns such as *me, you, him, her, us,* or *them* in place of Standard English reflexive pronouns *myself, yourself, himself, herself, ourselves,* or *themselves.*

Standard English	AAVE
He got *himself* a house.	He got *him* a house.
I made *myself* a sandwich.	I made *me* a sandwich.

Teach Explain to students that *myself, yourself, himself, herself, ourselves,* and *themselves* are special words that help emphasize who is receiving something in a sentence. Then write the following sentences on the board and read them aloud for students, emphasizing the underlined reflexive pronouns. Have students repeat after you.

> I got myself some lunch.　　He won himself a prize.
>
> They found themselves　　Get yourself a snack.
> some seats.

Practice Write these sentences on the board and read them aloud. Work with students to replace each underlined object pronoun with the Standard English reflexive pronoun, then have students read the new sentences aloud.

> She bought her a bicycle. (She bought herself a bicycle.)
>
> I got me a pet snake. (I got myself a pet snake.)
>
> We sang us to sleep. (We sang ourselves to sleep.)
>
> Find you a blanket. (Find yourself a blanket.)

Apply Have each student use *myself, yourself, himself, herself, ourselves,* or *themselves* in an oral or written sentence. Students can share their sentences with partners.

AAVE

Plural Constructions

In some cases, AAVE speakers may not use the plural *–s* with "nouns of measure" such as shown below. Additionally, AAVE speakers may need practice coordinating subject-verb agreement with plural constructions, especially in writing.

Standard English	AAVE
My lunch *costs two dollars*.	My lunch *cost two dollar*.
It *was six inches* long.	It *was six inch* long.
He has *two brothers*.	He *has two brother* or He *have two brother*.

Teach Explain to students that a plural noun is a word for more than one person, place, or thing. Most plural nouns in Standard English end with *–s* or *–es*. Tell students that they should pronounce these letters carefully when speaking and make sure to include them when writing. Also point out that the verb in a sentence must agree with the subject of a sentence (who or what the sentence is about), not a plural noun that comes after.

Write the following sentences on the board, read them aloud with emphasis on the plural endings, and have students repeat after you. Have students notice that each plural noun ends with *–s* or *–es* and that the verb in each sentence agrees with the subject.

> The toy costs fifty <u>cents</u>. The bag weighs 10 <u>pounds</u>.
>
> I have three <u>sisters</u>. Sean has two <u>sisters</u>.

Practice Write these sentences on the board and read them aloud. Work with students to fix the subject-verb agreement and change the underlined nouns to their plural form when needed. Point out that not all verbs and nouns need to be changed.

> He <u>pay</u> ten <u>dollar</u> each month. (He <u>pays</u> ten <u>dollars</u> each month.)
>
> I <u>have</u> two <u>basketball</u>. (I <u>have</u> two <u>basketballs</u>.)
>
> Alisha and her brother <u>make</u> two <u>lunch</u> each day. (Alisha and her brother <u>make</u> two <u>lunches</u> each day.)

Have students read the new sentences aloud.

Apply Have each student create an oral or written sentence about how much something costs, using Standard English plural constructions and subject-verb agreement. Have students share their sentences with partners.

Double Negatives

- The use of double negatives is a difficult tendency to overcome for many students, including some AAVE speakers. AAVE speakers are particularly likely to use negative inversions with double negatives, placing the subject of a sentence after a negative contraction such as *can't*. See the second and third examples below.

Standard English	AAVE
Nobody said *anything*.	*Nobody* said *nothing*.
Nobody can help.	*Can't nobody* help.
None are left or There *are none* left.	*Ain't none* left.

Teach Explain to students that it is not usually necessary to use more than one negative word, such as *no one, nobody, nothing, never, none, not,* or contractions with *not,* in a sentence. Then write the following sentence pairs on the board. Tell students that the negative words are underlined. The first sentence in each pair contains a double negative, while the second does not and is the appropriate Standard English form for use in school.

> I can't never finish on time. I can't ever finish on time.
> We don't have none. We don't have any.
> Isn't nobody here. Nobody is here.

Read each pair aloud and have students repeat the Standard English sentences. Have students notice that in the last example, the subject and verb in the sentences (*nobody* and *is*) are in a different order. In the Standard English version, the subject *nobody* is first.

Practice Write the following sentences on the board and read them aloud. Work with students to rewrite each sentence without the double negative. Point out that there may be more than one way to rewrite each sentence. Read the new sentences aloud as a group.

> Didn't nobody help.
> (Possible response: Nobody helped.)
>
> No one said nothing. (Possible response: No one said anything.)
>
> She hasn't never seen it.
> (Possible response: She hasn't seen it.)

Apply Have each student create a written or oral sentence describing something he or she has never done before. Tell them to incorporate negative words into their sentences and to use Standard English word order, but to avoid double negatives.

AAVE

Use of ain't

AAVE speakers may use ain't as a negative contraction in place of the Standard English *didn't, isn't, aren't, hasn't, haven't,* or *am not.* See the examples below.

Standard English	AAVE
They are not here or They aren't here.	They ain't here.
She did not do it or She didn't do it.	She ain't do it.
Ron has not finished or Ron hasn't finished.	Ron ain't finished.
I am not ready yet.	I ain't ready yet.

Teach Explain to students that Standard English uses several phrases and contractions that include the word *not,* including *did not (didn't), is not (isn't), are not (aren't), has not (hasn't), have not (haven't),* or *am not.* Write the following examples on the board, read them aloud, and have students repeat after you.

> We <u>aren't</u> allowed. They <u>didn't</u> stop.
> Mark <u>isn't</u> old enough. She <u>hasn't</u> been sick for years.
> I <u>am not</u> happy. The Browns <u>haven't</u> arrived.

Practice Write the following on the board. Work with students to change the underlined contraction in each to reflect Standard English usage. Read the new sentences aloud and have students repeat after you.

> I <u>ain't</u> mad. (I <u>am not</u> mad.)
> Kelly and Rick <u>ain't</u> here. (Kelly and Rick <u>aren't</u> here.)
> We <u>ain't</u> eaten yet. (We <u>haven't</u> eaten yet.)
> That backpack <u>ain't</u> mine. (That backpack <u>isn't</u> mine.)

Apply Write the following contractions on the board and have each student choose one to create a written or oral statement with. Have students share their work with their partners.

> didn't isn't aren't hasn't haven't am not

Writing

Writing Instruction

In *Houghton Mifflin Reading*, five-day instructional plans provide explicit instruction in writing modes, writing traits, and the writing process. Every theme also includes a Reading-Writing Workshop that gives students the opportunity to develop longer writing pieces. In addition, selected themes include Writing on Demand lessons that provide opportunities for timed writing.

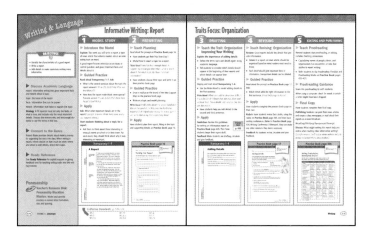

Writing Modes and Types

Houghton Mifflin Reading includes instruction in the following writing modes and types.

Examples of Writing Instruction in Grades 3–6
Summary
Description
Persuasive Writing • Opinion Essay • Book review • Letter to the Editor
Narrative Writing • Friendly Letter • Dialogue • Poem • Play • Fictional Narrative
Response to Literature • Journal Entry • Answering a Comprehension Question
Informative and Expository Writing • Explanation • Compare/Contrast Paragraph • Opinion Paragraph • Problem-Solution Essay • Business Letter • Report • Explanation • Biography

Writing

The Writing Process

Use this overview of the writing process as a reminder for yourself, or as an introduction for students, parents, or other adults in your classroom.

1. Prewriting

Prewriting includes choosing a topic, exploring the chosen topic, and organizing or planning the writing.

Choosing a Topic: If students aren't given a writing prompt, have them brainstorm a topic that they care about. They can think about experiences they have had or books they have read, or reread their journals. After listing several possible topics, have students discuss with you or with a partner which topic most interests them.

Exploring a Topic: Here are some strategies to teach students.

- **Brainstorm a list** of words and ideas about the topic.

- **Make a chart** of words and phrases about the topic for *sound, touch, sight, taste,* and *smell.*

- **Draw a picture.** As students think of details about the topic, have them add and label parts.

- **Talk with a partner** about the topic, purpose, audience, and how they will publish or share the writing. Make notes as new ideas come to you.

- **Use the five Ws.** Students can ask themselves *Who? What? When? Where? Why?* and *How?* about their topic.

Organizing Writing: Have students use a graphic organizer to put their details into separate groups. They should use the organization that fits best.

- **Time order.** Tell events in the order they happen.

- **Place order.** Describe details from top to bottom, right to left, or near to far.

- **Comparison and contrast.** Tell how two subjects are alike and different.

- **Order of importance.** Tell the least important or most important point or reason first.

- **Question and answer.** Ask a series of questions and tell the answers.

- **Another logical order.** Group details that belong together, and put them in an order that makes sense.

2. Drafting

When students are drafting, help them focus on getting their ideas down on paper. They can keep adding details, thinking as they go. They can cross out things they don't like and write down new ideas as they think of them. Tell students not to worry if their papers look messy or have mistakes. They should just keep writing! One good technique is to have students write on every other line so that they can make changes and fix mistakes later.

Share the following tips with students.

Write sentences and paragraphs. Use your graphic organizer. Each part of your plan should make a sentence or two if you're writing a single paragraph. Each part should make at least one paragraph in a longer piece. Most paragraphs will need a topic sentence that tells the main idea.

Write a beginning and an ending. Write an interesting beginning that introduces your topic. Write an ending that summarizes it or makes a final comment about it.

Make connections. Use connecting, or transitional, words such as *then* and *also* to tie your sentences and paragraphs together.

3. Revising

Revising is changing writing to make it clearer or more interesting. Have students start by making changes on their draft. Here are some strategies students can use as they review and revise their drafts.

Look at a rubric or checklist. Does your draft cover all the writing traits? Let the rubric guide you in making changes.

Ask yourself questions. If you don't have a rubric, ask yourself these questions.

- Did I write clear topic sentences?
- Did I use details that explain the topic sentence in each paragraph?
- Did I order the details so my readers can follow them easily?
- Where do I need to add sense words or details?
- Does my writing sound right for my audience and purpose?
- Did I make a final comment about my topic in my ending?

Have a writing conference. Meet with a partner, a small group, or your teacher.

4. Proofreading

Proofreading is correcting mistakes. Students should check spelling, capitalization, and punctuation. They should also make sure that they have used words correctly, written complete sentences, and indented paragraphs.

Students can use the following ideas to help them proofread.

- Use proofreading marks.
- Proofread for one skill at a time.
- Read one line at a time. Hold a ruler or strip of cardboard under the line to help you focus on the spelling of each word.
- Say each word aloud to yourself.
- Read your paper aloud. You may notice mistakes when you hear them.
- Circle any word that might be misspelled. Check spelling in a dictionary.

5. Publishing

Publishing is preparing your writing to share it with an audience. Share the following ideas with students.

Write It

- Turn you paper into a book. Add pictures and a cover.
- Send your paper as a letter or an e-mail.
- Create a class book of writing with your classmates.
- Post your paper on the Internet.
- Send your paper to a magazine or a newspaper that publishes student writing.

Writing

The Writing Process

Say It

- Record your paper on tape. Add sound effects.
- Read your paper aloud from the Author's Chair.
- Read your paper as a speech.

Show It

- Show slides about your topic to the class while reading your paper aloud.
- Add photographs, diagrams, charts, graphs, or drawings to your paper.
- Act out your writing with a small group. Have a teacher or other adult videotape your performance.

Writing Traits

Use this overview of writing traits as a reminder for yourself, or as an introduction for students, parents, or other adults in your classroom.

Ideas

Ideas are the thoughts, feelings, or facts that you put into words. Those ideas come through clearly when you use clear details. Suppose you are writing about a boy who is stuck inside on a rainy day. What details make up that idea? They might include the raindrops on the window, the sound of a ticking clock, and the boy's thoughts about how bored he feels. As you write, think about the details that best express your ideas.

Organization

Every piece of writing is like a journey, with a beginning, middle, and end. The organization is how you plan the route. A historical report might be organized like a time line, from the earliest events to the most recent. A mystery story might have a detective finding a series of clues. Use a graphic organizer or an outline to organize your ideas before you write. Each important idea or event should have its own paragraph.

Sentence Fluency

Words don't just contain meaning; they have sound and rhythm, too. Sentence fluency is the way your writing sounds to the ear. Do the sentences flow smoothly? Are they all the same, or do they show variety? How does the writing sound when you read it aloud? When you revise your writing, you can change sentences so they sound more natural and are easier to read.

Voice

Every writer has a special voice that is like no one else's. When you read a favorite author, you probably know that author's tone, sense of humor, or style of sentences. It all adds up to the author's voice. What is your voice like? Do you use a lot of description? Is your language simple but clear? Do your words shout or sing? Just as your speaking voice shows who you are, so does your writing voice.

Word Choice

To get your ideas across in your writing, you need to choose the right words. Sometimes simple words work better than fancy words. Sometimes there's one word that's exactly right. If you want to describe a particular shade of blue, *indigo* might be a better choice than *blue*. Which words express the face of a girl who has just eaten a delicious spoonful of ice cream? The more words you know, the surer your choice!

Conventions

Sometimes we take them for granted—spelling, grammar, capital letters, and punctuation. They are the conventions of writing, and if they're wrong or mixed up, the best ideas and word choices won't get through to the reader. That's why good writers always do a careful check to make sure the spelling, grammar, and other conventions help the message and don't confuse it.

Ready Reference

Instructional Routine for Focusing on Form

As students move through the intermediate grades—especially Grade 6—they will need to focus on which form of writing best suits their intended purpose. They write to inform, to explain, to narrate, to entertain, to persuade, to describe, to express themselves—purposes that may be achieved in many cases via multiple formats. The Focusing on Form Strategy can help

students explore the usefulness of various writing forms and formats and the effect of format on aspects of their writing.

In *Houghton Mifflin Reading*, your students will have multiple opportunities to write in a number of writing modes and formats. This routine helps students to recognize and explore different ways of approaching writing activities.

Focusing on Form in Writing

TEACHER	Grade 6 Examples	STUDENTS
Read the **Responding** page writing activity.	*Pages 44, 66, 110, 158, 266, 402, 424, 490, 512, 564*	
Model the task. Show students that the purpose for writing is separate from the form it takes.	*The writing activity on page 44 is about explaining. You could write a paragraph or two explaining your point of view, but your explanation could also be in the form of a letter to a friend, or a newspaper article.*	
Guide students to suggest forms and formats the activity could take.	*In what other form could this explanation be written?*	Suggest forms and formats. It could be an Internet blog on survival skills or even a journal entry.
Have students choose the form in which they will complete the assignment.	*In which format can you best explain your point of view?*	Choose a format.
After students complete the assignment, have them share and compare the forms or formats they used.	*How did the form you chose affect your writing? Was your tone formal or informal? Did you make different word choices?*	Share and compare their explanations.
In the **Day 5 Writing lesson**, discuss with students what other forms of writing would suit the week's writing purpose.	*This week you wrote a specified form of writing, a book review [for example]. What was the overall purpose of your writing?*	Answer: To persuade [for example].
Model thinking of other writing forms and formats that persuasive writing could take.	*I could persuade a friend to read the book by writing a friendly letter.*	
Expand the discussion.	*If you wanted to convince people to share your point of view on an issue at school or in the news, what form could that persuasive writing take?*	Suggest other forms: a letter to the editor, an editorial in the school paper, a speech.

Assessment

See pages 82–83 for a complete overview of the five-step California Assessment Plan.
The plan includes the following assessment tools.

Starting Out...	• Comprehensive Screening test • Diagnostic Assessment
For Every Theme...	• Weekly Skills Tests • Theme Skills Tests • Integrated Theme Tests
Periodically, or at Year's End...	• California Summative Tests • California Assessments

Theme 1

Five Steps that Work Together

California Assessment Plan

Beginning of the Year	Every Day

① Where Do I Start?

Comprehensive Screening Assessment

- Group-administered test
- Initial screening of previous year's skills: Language Arts, Phonics/Decoding, and Writing, plus passages for Comprehension and Vocabulary
- Includes an optional group Spelling test

Diagnostic Assessment

- Individually administered test, for struggling readers only
- Diagnosis of basic reading skills, plus passages for reading in context
- Can be re-administered later in year to document individual progress

What Happens...

② Every Day?

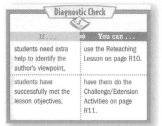

Diagnostic Check

- Monitor progress
- Differentiate instruction successfully

Corrective Feedback

- Provide immediate and helpful feedback

Technology

Edusoft
A Houghton Mifflin Company

Online **Assessment System**

| Every Week | Every Theme | End of the Year |

3 Every Week?

Weekly Skills Tests

- Group-administered
- Monitor the development of specific Vocabulary, Reading, and Language Arts skills

Observation Checklists
- Record student progress on weekly objectives. See **Teacher's Resource Blackline Masters**.

4 Every Theme?

Theme Skills Tests

- Group-administered
- Measure the theme's reading and writing skills

Integrated Theme Tests

- Group-administered; integrate reading and language arts

5 Periodically, Year's End?

California Summative Tests

- Group-administered
- Comprehensive, measure the year's ELA standards in preparation for California Standards Tests at grades 2–6

California Assessments

- Assess Fluency, Writing, and Novel Unit skills; provide practice with California Standards Test formats

 Administer online tests.
Get instant results online or by scan-and-score.

 Report performance on your California standards.

 Get recommendations for differentiating instruction and intervention.

Notes

Additional Resources

Activities

Alliteration
Have students write phrases, sentences, and poems that use alliteration. Students can choose a sound from the Sound/Spelling Cards or the sound can be assigned. As the year progresses, you can post their writing below the corresponding Sound/Spelling Cards.

Hear the Sound, Write the Words
Have students work in pairs. One student holds 4 or 5 Sound/Spelling Cards without letting the partner see them. The first student says the sound. The second student writes down a spelling for the sound and as many words that begin with that sound as possible in one minute. Students then switch roles after each card. Then they share their lists.

Fill-in-the-Blank Stories
Have students work in pairs. Have each student write a half-page short story, and then ask students to erase all of the nouns from their story. Give each pair of students a Sound/Spelling Card. Tell students to take turns asking their partner for nouns that contain that sound, to complete each story. Then have them read their stories to each other.

Advanced Have students erase all nouns, verbs, and adjectives from their stories and repeat the activity.

Common Sounds
Organize students into small groups. Write four random letters on the board where they can be seen easily. Challenge groups to write down as many words as possible that contain all of the letters.

Struggling Readers After writing four random letters on the board, ask the groups to write as many words as possible that begin with the letters.

Advanced Use Sound/Spelling Cards for the activity. Ask students to write words that contain all of the sounds and their spellings.

Definition Matching
Select a Sound/Spelling Card and show it to the class. Have each student list ten words that begin with that sound. Arrange students in pairs. Have one student say the definition of one of their words to their partner. Have the partner guess the word. If the partner cannot guess the word, have the first student rephrase the definition until the partner guesses correctly.

Secret Sound Codes
Arrange students in pairs. Have each student write a secret message to his or her partner on a sheet of paper. Then, have students make up a secret code—one in which a number represents each sound used in the words of their secret message. Have students use the Sound/Spelling Cards to identify each of the sounds that will require a number. Have students use their code to rewrite their message in number form. Ask students to give their number message, along with the key to their code, to their partners. Have students decode their partner's message.

Struggling Readers Have students participate in the activity as described above, but create a secret code for them to use.

Sound Descriptions
Give a Sound/Spelling Card to each student. Ask each student to list adjectives that contain that sound and that describe a certain item in the classroom. Ask a few students to share their adjective list with the class to see whether their classmates can guess the mystery item being described.

Same Letter, Different Sounds
Provide each student with a short article from an old newspaper or magazine. Give each student a letter. Have students read through the article and circle all the words in which that letter is used. Have each student list the sounds that are made by that letter in the circled words.

Sound Art
Assign a Sound/Spelling Card to each student. On a sheet of paper, have each student write words that show all the spelling combinations for that sound. Then, have students further explain their examples by drawing a picture that represents each of the example words.

Best Practices for Your Sound/Spelling Cards

HOUGHTON MIFFLIN

1049695

Purpose of the Sound/Spelling Cards

This set of 47 **Sound/Spelling Cards** helps students learn and remember the connections between the sounds in English and their written forms. Each card shows a picture whose name contains a focus sound along with the most common spellings for the sound. All sound spellings on these cards are taught in *Houghton Mifflin Journeys*.

Each card has two sides, one with a green border and one with an orange border. The side with the green border includes all the sound spellings introduced in Grade 4, and the side with the orange border includes all the sound spellings introduced in Grades 5 and 6. Use self-stick notes to cover new spellings until you're ready to teach them.

Use the **Sound/Spelling Cards** as a resource to introduce, reinforce, and review the various sounds and their related spelling patterns. Display the **Large Sound/Spelling Cards** in the classroom to help students in their independent reading and writing. Distribute the **Small Sound/Spelling Cards** to students as they work in small groups or independently.

Structure of the Sound/Spelling Cards

The name of the picture on each card stands for a distinct sound in English. The most common letter or letter combination used to spell the sound appears below the picture. Note that voiced vowels appear in red, unvoiced in black. In addition, colored bands signal distinct vowel sounds: green for short vowels, yellow for long vowels, blue for vowel pairs. Note also that some letter combinations include a blank line. These lines indicate where in a syllable that particular spelling usually appears. The blank in _ck, for instance, shows that ck usually comes at the end of a syllable.

Management Tips

1. Plan
★ Make Sound/Spelling Cards available for students to use during reading and writing activities and in Small Group time.

★ Model each activity for students. Introduce new activities to the class before having small groups perform them.

★ Limit participation in a given activity by assigning students to specific groups before beginning a Sound/Spelling Cards activity. Do not designate groups that exceed the size specified for each activity.

2. Engage
★ As you interact with students and use the prompts during these activities, note oral language and problem-solving skills of individual students.

★ Near the end of a given week, remind students that they may review the material that has been covered by repeating the Sound/Spelling activities that have been used during the week.

★ Refresh activities that have already been done by incorporating new sounds and words as the students learn them. If students initially participated in a regular activity, try introducing the Advanced version of the same activity.

✓ **Observing Students** Note in your daily records which students are assigned to each activity. Keeping accurate records will ensure that you observe each student for proper evaluation.

3. Reflect
★ Have students tell what they learned after each activity. They can help select samples of their writing from these activities for their permanent portfolios. Have them mark each item with a date to show progress over time.

★ When students are familiar with the Sound/Spelling Cards, allow them to suggest future activities that they may enjoy.

Sound/Spelling Card Routine
Purpose Use this Routine to provide students with the opportunity to learn and review sound/symbol relationships.

Introduce a Sound/Spelling Card

TEACHER		STUDENTS
Display **Sound/Spelling Card**.	m _mb _lm	Observe.
Say the sound and name the card as you point to the picture.	Listen: /m/ mouse Now you say it.	/m/ mouse
• Point to and name the sound and spelling(s). • Have students name the sound and spelling(s) three times.	Listen: /m/ . . . m /m/ . . . m /m/ . . . m m _mb _lm Now you say it.	/m/ . . . m /m/ . . . m /m/ . . . m
Display and read words as you point out the spelling of the target sound in the word.	Look: mat mat starts with m /m/	Observe.
Read the word again, and have students read it with you. Repeat with one or two more example words.	Listen: mat Now you say it.	mat
Repeat for alternative spellings for the sound, if appropriate.		

Review a Sound/Spelling Card
Practice and review at random, as necessary.

TEACHER		STUDENTS
Touch the picture on the card.	What is the picture on the card?	mouse
Point to the sound on the card.	What is the sound?	/m/
Point to the spelling on the card.	What is the spelling?	m

Language Transfer Charts

Positive Transfer

Not every aspect of every language differs from English. Those languages that share the closest historical ties with English naturally have many areas of positive transfer. One of the most important areas of positive transfer is the alphabet that we share with many of the European languages. The following list describes some general areas of positive language transfer.

Shared alphabet	A shared alphabet gives students an advantage over those who must learn a new alphabet.
Shared historical development	The shared historical development of the European languages allows students to make analogies with their own language.
Cognates	Cognates allow students to make fairly accurate guesses about meaning even though false cognates are likely to mislead students.
Similar sounds	Similar sounds occur in many languages.
Language structures	Many language structures in English occur in other languages as well.
Writing conventions	Some writing conventions apply in related languages.
Figurative language	Languages tend to use figurative language to express similar ideas even though the exact words vary considerably.

Transfer Errors

On the following pages you'll find two kinds of charts.

The **Language Guide to Transfer Errors** on pages 88–91 describes the types of grammatical errors you might encounter in teaching students from different language backgrounds. The languages cited include those most common in California schools (Spanish, Vietnamese, Tagalog, Cantonese, and Hmong), as well as 18 others.

The **Consonant Sounds, Consonant Cluster,** and **Vowel Sounds** charts on pages 92–94 identify sounds that English language learners may have difficulty discerning. Students may hear different words as similar or may not easily recognize spoken words.

Additional Resources

Language Guide to Transfer Errors

The following language guide sets out several problem areas for students acquiring English. It shows grammatical features *(column 1)* of specific languages *(column 2)* that when transferred to English lead to an error *(column 3)*. The guide covers neither all linguistic problem areas nor all languages; that would take volumes. Rather, it lists a selection, with the aim of being useful and practical. Use the guide to raise your awareness about languages.

LANGUAGE FEATURES / LANGUAGES / SAMPLE TRANSFER ERRORS IN ENGLISH

ARTICLES	Arabic	Bengali	Chinese	Farsi	French	German	Gujarati	Greek	Haitian Creole	Hebrew	Hindi	Hmong	Japanese	Khmer	Korean	Portuguese	Russian	Spanish	Swahili	Tagalog	Thai	Turkish	Urdu	Vietnamese	ARTICLES (Sample transfer errors in English)
No articles		●	●									●					●		●	●		●	●		Book is on table. Sun is hot.
No indefinite article with profession				●	●			●				●			●									●	He is student. She doctor.
Definite article with days, months, places, idioms	●						●																		She is at the home. They will come in the July.
Definite article used for generalization	●				●											●	●	●							The little children always like the ice cream. The swimming is good exercise.
No article for generalization with singular noun																									Bird can fly.
Definite article used with proper noun				●	●		●	●								●	●	●							My dentist is the Doctor Smith.
No definite article										●											●				Store on corner is closed.
No indefinite article (uses *one* for *a* and depends on context)														●	●										He found one book.

From *Houghton Mifflin English: Students Acquiring English Practice Book* by Templeton, et al. Chart adapted from *Keys for Writers*, Second Edition by Ann Raimes. Copyright © 1999, 2001 by Houghton Mifflin Company. Reprinted by permission of Houghton Mifflin Company. All rights reserved.

LANGUAGES — VERBS AND VERBALS

VERBS AND VERBALS	Example	Arabic	Bengali	Chinese	Farsi	French	German	Gujarati	Greek	Haitian Creole	Hebrew	Hindi	Hmong	Japanese	Khmer	Korean	Portuguese	Russian	Spanish	Swahili	Tagalog	Thai	Turkish	Urdu	Vietnamese
Be can be omitted	She studying now. / He always happy.	●		●					●								●								
No progressive forms	They still play now. / When I called, she studied.		●		●	●		●									●								
No tense inflections	He have a good time yesterday. / When she was little, she always walk to school.		●	●																	●				●
No inflections for person and number	The school have a good soccer team.		●	●					●				●		●		●				●				●
Past perfect formed with be	They were arrived.	●																							
Different tense boundaries from English	I study English for a year. / He has left yesterday.	●	●	●	●				●																
Different limits for passive voice	They were taken our lunches. My name base on Chinese characters. An accident was happened.												●	●	●		●				●				●
No -ing (gerund)/infinitive distinction	She avoids to see him. / I enjoy to play baseball.	●	●	●	●			●								●		●							●
Infinitive not used to express purpose	I went out for seeing a movie.														●										
Overuse of progressive forms	I am wanting to leave now.											●												●	

LANGUAGE TRANSFER CHARTS: LANGUAGE GUIDE TO TRANSFER ERRORS, *CONTINUED*

WORD ORDER AND SENTENCE STRUCTURE

WORD ORDER AND SENTENCE STRUCTURE	Arabic	Bengali	Chinese	Farsi	French	German	Gujarati	Greek	Haitian Creole	Hebrew	Hindi	Hmong	Japanese	Khmer	Korean	Portuguese	Russian	Spanish	Swahili	Tagalog	Thai	Turkish	Urdu	Vietnamese	WORD ORDER AND SENTENCE STRUCTURE (examples)
Verb precedes subject	•								•							•	•		•						*Good grades received every student in the class.*
Verb–subject order in dependent clause	•			•	•			•																	*Spanish: optional*
Verb last		•				•				•	•		•	•	•						•				*I knew what would say the teacher.*
Coordination favored over subordination	•																								*...when the teacher the papers collected.* / *German: in dependent clause* / *Frequent use of and and so*
Relative clause or restrictive phrase precedes noun it modifies		•	•									•	•	•	•										*The entered in the contest students... / He gave me a too difficult for me book.*
Adverb can occur between verb and object or before verb								•						•											*I like very much oranges. / She watched carefully the baby. / He slowly runs.*
That clause rather than infinitive								•		•				•		•	•								*Urdu: before verb*
Inversion of subject and verb rare		•		•																					*I want that you stay. / Father wants that he try harder.*
Conjunctions occur in pairs		•	•																						*She is leaving and so I am.*
Subject can be omitted (especially pronoun)												•	•			•	•			•					*Although she is rich, but she drives an old car. Even if I had time, I would also not go.* / *Is raining. / Studied last night.*
Commas set off a dependent clause					•											•									*He knows, that we called.*
No equivalent of *there is/there are*												•	•	•	•	•	•			•					*This book says four reasons to eat beans. / In the park has many trees.* / *Thai: uses adverb of place and have*

LANGUAGES

NOUNS, PRONOUNS, ADJECTIVES, ADVERBS	Vietnamese	Urdu	Turkish	Thai	Tagalog	Swahili	Spanish	Russian	Portuguese	Korean	Khmer	Japanese	Hmong	Hindi	Hebrew	Haitian Creole	Greek	Gujarati	German	French	Farsi	Chinese	Bengali	Arabic	NOUNS, PRONOUNS, ADJECTIVES, ADVERBS
Personal pronouns restate subject							●												●					●	*My grandfather he lives in California.*
No human/nonhuman distinction for relative pronoun (who/which)					●		●	●	●												●	●		●	*Here is the new student which you met her last week. The people which arrived...*
Pronoun object added at end of relative clause																●						●		●	*The house that I used to live in it is big.*
No distinction between subject and object forms of pronouns					●		●				●								●			●	●		*I gave the books to she.*
Nouns and adjectives have the same form													●										●		*She is very beauty woman. They felt very safety on the bus.*
No distinction between he/she, his/her					●														●						*My sister dropped his lunch.*
No plural form after a number											●											●			*Four new shirt...*
No plural (or optional) forms of nouns					●						●		●										●		*Several good book...*
No relative pronouns											●														*The book is on the table is mine.*
Adjectives show number							●														●				*I have helpfuls friends.*
Double negatives are routinely used							●																		*They don't know nothing.*
Pronoun subjects can be omitted					●		●	●																	*My mother complained when saw the mess.*

LANGUAGE TRANSFER CHARTS
Sounds

Consonant Sounds

Consonant sounds in English present different challenges to different populations of English language learners. For example, although Chinese, Vietnamese, and Khmer are not related languages, speakers of these languages often have difficulty hearing and spelling sounds in English. In particular, consonants and consonant clusters present difficulties for these learners. In addition, because a modified Roman alphabet is used in Vietnamese, children who read and write that language may have difficulty when English sounds and letters are introduced. The chart on page C12 provides information and support for helping students master English consonant sounds.

Consonant Clusters

Consonant clusters (combinations of consonant sounds, as in *splashed* and *strength)* often pose problems for English language learners. Depending on their primary language, students might

- add a vowel sound before a consonant cluster at the beginning of a word (for example, pronounce *student* as "estudent").
- simplify the cluster by dropping the last consonant (for example, drop the *z* sound at the end of *dogs*)
- insert a vowel between consonants in a cluster (for example, pronounce *price* as "pi-rice" or "pe-rice.")
- substitute for an unfamiliar consonant cluster a similar one that exists only in their primary language (for example, Hmong has many consonant clusters that do not exist in English)

Vowel Sounds

English vowel sounds present students with many challenges. In general, learners whose primary language has fewer vowel sounds than English may not be sensitive to some meaningful differences among vowel sounds in English. That is, they may not hear such sounds as the long *e* in *eat* and the short *i* in *it* as indicating two different words.

In contrast, learners whose primary language has **more** vowel sounds than English may be confused by differences among vowel sounds that are not meaningful to English speakers, such as differences due to regional accents.

The chart on page C13 provides help in understanding some difficulties students might have with English vowels.

Consonant Sounds

Consonant Sound	Arabic	Chinese	Hmong	Khmer	Russian	Spanish	Vietnamese
/b/		beginning	•		end	end	end
/ch/							•
/d/		beginning			end	end	end
/f/				•			•
/g/	•	beginning	•	•	end	end	end
/h/					•	•	
/hw/				•			
/j/			•	•		•	•
/k/					beginning	beginning	•
/kw/							
/l/							beginning
/m/							
/n/							
/ng/	•				•		
/p/	•				beginning	beginning	beginning
/r/	•	•					
/s/							end
/sh/				•		•	•
/t/					beginning	beginning	beginning
/th/	•			•	•		•
/th/	•	•		•	•	•	•
/v/	•	•				•	end
/w/					•		
/y/						•	
/z/		•		•		•	•

Additional Resources

Vowel Sounds

Language	Features
Arabic	Arabic has only eight vowel sounds and diphthongs as compared to over 20 in English. Learners may gloss over and confuse short vowel sounds in English. Learners may add glottal stops (as in the middle of "uh-oh") before words beginning with vowel sounds.
Chinese	Chinese has fewer vowel sounds than English. Chinese is a tonal language. Each syllable is pronounced with a particular tone (for example, high or low pitch, rising or falling pitch, and so on) that gives it meaning. Thus it is not just the combination of vowel and consonant sounds that forms a particular word, but also its tone. Learners may have trouble reducing an unstressed vowel to a schwa; they may either give it too much stress or omit it.
Hmong	Hmong has six pure vowels and seven diphthongs (fewer vowel sounds than English has). Hmong is a tonal language. Each syllable is pronounced with a particular tone (for example, high or low pitch, rising or falling pitch, and so on) that gives it meaning. Thus it is not just the combination of vowel and consonant sounds that forms a particular word, but also its tone.
Khmer	Khmer has 16 vowel sounds and 11 diphthongs (more than English has). Learners may have trouble with short vowel sounds that do not exist in Khmer (as in *bat, bet,* and *bit).* Learners may confuse long and short vowel sounds (as in *seat* and *set).*
Russian	There are no diphthongs in Russian. Learners will probably have difficulty pronouncing /ûr/, especially after *w,* as in *work.* Learners may shorten long vowels (*field* becomes *filled, seat* becomes *sit).* The short *a* sound may become short *e* (*sat* becomes *set).*
Spanish	Spanish has five pure vowel sounds and five diphthongs (fewer than English has). The sounds of long *e* (as in *sheep)* and short *i* (as in *ship)* are often confused; the same is true of the sounds of long *oo* (as in *pool)* and short *oo* (as in *book* or *pull).* The schwa sound in English words is often replaced by the strong pronunciation of the vowel; about becomes ä´bout´.
Vietnamese	The Vietnamese vowel system is complex, with 11 pure vowels and many more diphthongs and triphthongs. Learners may simplify long vowels in English (such as the long *o* in *low* and the long *a* in *may)* to their pure Vietnamese counterparts. Variations in the length of vowels (according to individual English speaker's accent) may confuse learners since such variations carry different meanings in Vietnamese.

OUR RESEARCH

> "No one test or assessment should be asked to serve all the assessment purposes. We need, at this point, a system made up of articulated components, glued together by their adherence to content standards and serving explicit purposes for assessment."
>
> — *National Council for Education Standards and Testing, 1992*

Understanding Assessment: Putting Together the Puzzle

Sheila W. Valencia

As far back as 1992, when the standards movement was launched, the National Council for Education Standards and Testing, a team of experts in education, assessment, and policy, reminded our nation of the different purposes for assessment—from public accountability to creating individualizing instructional plans for children. They also cautioned us to use multiple measures to fit these purposes including standardized tests, running records, informal reading inventories, classroom projects, portfolios, writing samples, debates, literature circle discussions, and more. Now, 10 years later, we are hearing the same reminder (Brennan, Kim, Wenz-Gross, Siperstein, 2001; Herman, 2001; International Reading Association, 1999). In fact, in July 2001 members of the National Education Association, the nation's largest teacher's union, endorsed a policy calling for a combination of standardized tests and other assessment tools such as teacher designed assessments when making important educational decisions (Blair & Archer, 2001).

Assessment has always been a part of the educational landscape. However, because assessment can serve so many different purposes and can come in so many different forms, it has been confusing and, sometimes, it has been the subject of contentious debate. Unfortunately, as a result, many of us have come to view assessment as a necessary evil, a requirement rather than a helpful part of instruction. But assessment IS a critical part of instruction and it CAN be useful if we understand the pieces of the puzzle.

A Balanced Approach to Assessment

A balanced assessment system consists of three parts (see Figure 1): standard assessment, classroom-based assessment, and student self-assessment.

Each of these parts serves a different purpose and each is a different and important piece of the puzzle.

Standard Assessment

Standard assessment is the term we use here to refer to assessments that are given to all students in a state, school district, or school. We used to think of these simply as norm-referenced tests, such as the Stanford Achievement Test or the Gates-MacGinitie Reading Test, that compare student performance to the performance of a national sample of students at the same grade. But these days, many states have constructed their own tests, such as the ISAT in Illinois, the FCAT in Florida,

Figure 1

or the direct writing assessment in California, that are not norm-referenced. Instead, they have used criteria for student performance set by the state. Regardless of whether a state uses a norm-referenced test or a state-developed test, these standard assessments are designed to evaluate students in a uniform, systematic way against some established standard. All 50 states now administer some type of standard assessment to students at targeted grade levels (Orlofsky & Olson, 2001).

There are cautions to keep in mind related to standard assessments. First, although familiarizing students with the test format is important, studies indicate that if students only practice with the format of a test, they are less likely to actually learn (Linn, 2000; Popham, 1999). Preparing students to do well involves more than test preparation; it involves helping students learn to apply important reading and writing strategies.

A second caution relates to interpreting test scores. Standard assessments, by their very nature, are not precise, but rather rough approximations of student performance (Popham, 1999). Furthermore, they are not good measures of students who are performing substantially below or above their grade placement. For example, most of the reading selections on a standard reading assessment designed for fourth-grade students would be at the third, fourth, or fifth-grade level. It would be unlikely for such a test to include passages at first or second grade level or at eighth or ninth grade level. As a result, students who are reading at these levels will be unable to demonstrate their abilities on the standard grade-level test. What's more, even if these students were to make gains from September to June, it would be very difficult to show gains using these tests—they simply don't have enough items at the lower and higher levels.

Finally, recent surveys have documented that only 10 of 50 states provide teachers or students with feedback on how individual students perform on particular

Additional Resources

test items found on standard assessments (Education Week, 2001). They simply provide overall scores, and often they provide those scores after students have moved on to another grade and another teacher. Boser (2001) concludes that "states rarely provide feedback needed for teachers and students to learn from their mistakes." So, the lack of specific and timely feedback makes it unlikely that teachers or students could use the results to direct future learning. In summary, standard assessments provide important systematic information about student learning in relation to other students or to a pre-established standard of performance. This information is particularly useful to people outside of the classroom such as legislators and administrators. Standard assessments work much like a thermometer, taking students' temperature to evaluate their academic health or abilities. However, thermometers don't help us know exactly what is causing our illness or how to get better. For that we need finer-grained assessments and well-trained physicians. That's where classroom-based assessment comes into play.

Classroom-based Assessment

In the past several years, classroom-based assessment has enjoyed renewed support from policymakers (i.e. National Research Council, 1999), assessment experts (Shepard, 1999), and teachers (International Reading Association, 1999) alike, giving it a central position in all assessment discussions. **Recent studies suggest that teachers, themselves, are the most important assessment tool.** This makes perfect sense when you realize that teachers spend 1/3 to 1/2 of their classroom time in assessment-related activities (Stiggins & Conklin, 1992) and that they make decisions about what and how to teach

approximately every 2–3 minutes (Shavelson & Stern, 1981)!

Teachers must be able to develop assessment strategies, gather evidence, analyze what they see, and ultimately, make instructional adjustments to

> **Teachers become more focused on what and how to teach, and students become more self-directed, motivated, and focused on learning...**

respond to student needs. This is precisely why classroom assessment is so powerful. Classroom-based assessment is conducted close to actual learning and to children; as a result, it is most likely to be aligned with instruction, provide immediate feedback to teachers and students, engage students in assessment of their learning, and influence instructional decisions. Classroom assessment also occurs more frequently than standard or norm-referenced testing, and it can be more precisely tailored to individual children and to instruction. With classroom-based assessment, assessment and instruction are melded. Both teachers and students become learners. Teachers become more focused on what and how to teach, and students become more self-directed, motivated, and focused on learning (Graue, 1993; Wolf, 1989).

Classroom-based assessment includes a wide range of tools and strategies. Because the assessments grow out of actual classroom activities, they are more likely to resemble authentic reading and writing and standard assessments (Hiebert, Valencia & Afflerbach, 1994; Wiggins, 1993). For example, students might demonstrate their literacy abilities by conducting research and writing a report, developing a character analysis, debating a character's motives, dramatizing a favorite story, drawing and writing about a nonfiction piece, or reading aloud and discussing a portion of text with the teacher. These assessments can range from relatively short assessments to long-term projects. They often require students to apply their skills and strategies to new reading and writing tasks, and they often value the thinking behind work—the process—as much as the finished product (Pearson & Valencia, 1987; Wiggins, 1989; Wolf, 1989).

Just because assessment is conducted in the classroom, doesn't make it good assessment. Research suggests that classroom assessment must have three critical features. First, it must be aligned with instruction. Although this seems obvious, teachers sometimes inadvertently hold students accountable for things they haven't adequately taught or students haven't adequately practiced (Valencia, 1998). At the same time, teachers must make decisions about the most important things to assess rather than treating all learning as equally valuable (Wiggins, 1989). There is nothing worse than collecting lots of information that you don't use or that targets unimportant learning. Classroom time is too precious to waste. So, teachers must be strategic and focused as they implement class-

types of assessments over time will ensure that students are provided with ample opportunities to demonstrate their abilities and that teachers' conclusions are well-founded.

Student Self-Assessment

Student self-assessment may seem like an extravagant addition to the assessment system, however, both scholars and classroom experience suggest that it is an important piece of the puzzle. Students who are engaged in self-assessment do not become dependent on teachers to determine how well they are doing or where they need more work (Reif, 1990). They see learning as within their control and gain a sense of responsibility and ownership. They move from passive learners (Johnston & Winograd, 1985), unengaged and uninspired, to active learners. As a result, these students become more focused on their work. They learn the qualities of good work, how to judge their work against those qualities, and how to assess their own efforts and feelings of accomplishment (Reif, 1990; Wolf, 1989). They are more likely to set goals and to accomplish them, and consequently, their learning improves (Andrade, 2000; Stiggins, 1997). These students are also more likely to share common goals and expectations with their teachers (Valencia, 1998). That means that teachers and students can work together, rather than at cross-purposes, because they have a shared understanding of what they want to accomplish.

We caution that self-assessment can sometimes overemphasize superficial aspects of students' work (i.e. handwriting, drawings), efforts (i.e. I worked hard), or unexamined feelings (i.e. I like it, it's good). In fact, studies sug-

room assessment. State and district curriculum guides, published instructional materials, national standards documents, and professional colleagues are good resources for determining important learning outcomes for students (Education Week, 2001; Valencia & Place, 1994).

Classroom assessment also needs to be ongoing. This implies that teachers must continually re-evaluate student learning and then use that information to adjust instruction.

Finally, good classroom assessment must rely on a variety of forms of assessment. For some students, written work is difficult, so too much reliance on written work will put them at a disadvantage (Jenkins, Johnson & Hileman, 2000). Similarly, particular activities or topics will inspire excellent performance in some students and frustrate others. And, work supported by teachers or completed collaboratively with peers may give a different impression of students' capabilities than work completed independently. Including a variety of

Additional Resources

gest that without support to go beyond the superficial, students tend not to develop a more reflective and analytic stance toward their learning (Valencia, 1998). A related caution is that self-assessment can easily become routine and uninspired if it is overused or used in the same way regardless of the kind of work. Students can grow as weary of self-assessment as any mundane activity. The antidote for such problems is to provide instruction in self-assessment (modeling, guidance, practice), time (self-assessment cannot be rushed), and many opportunities for students to discuss insights about their own learning. Like any skill or strategy, self-assessment needs support to develop.

How Can Teachers Become More Effective at Balanced Assessment?

Compared to a jigsaw puzzle, it may not seem difficult to put together only three pieces of the assessment puzzle. But, it is. On one hand, we must struggle continually to overcome tradition and the current inclination to rely on a single, standard score. As educators, we need to counter the illusion of a simple score and the almost exclusive confidence those outside education ascribe to standard assessments. On the other hand, we must learn to deal with multiple indicators (i.e. indicators from standard, classroom-based, and student self-assessment as well as multiple indicators within each type of assessment). Sometimes information from multiple sources will converge, providing a consistent evaluation of student performance; other times the information may be discrepant because of differences in assessment formats, the skills and strategies tested, or simply inconsistencies in student learning. But, it is important to value all the information and to remem-

ber that the more samples of student learning we collect, the more trustworthy and informative our results.

We close with several suggestions for implementing the pieces of a balanced assessment system.

- When making important educational decisions or sharing information with parents, be sure to use information from all three pieces—standard assessment, classroom assessment, and student self-assessment. Be sure you understand the purpose and focus of each assessment as well as the strengths and limitations of each. Help parents understand them as well. Use the information to describe students' strengths and needs, rather than to label them with a grade or a number, and to plan for instruction.

> ... it is important to value all the information and to remember that the more samples of student learning we collect, the more trustworthy and informative our results.

- Focus assessment on the most important outcomes in the curriculum. Although teachers informally assess every time they interact with students and every time students work on an activity, you do not have to

document every interaction or every lesson. Daily lessons and activities are often building blocks to more complex goals. Determine the most important goals you have for each unit. Then select a couple of artifacts or focal points for your anecdotal notes or checklists. Use these assessments judiciously depending on the situation, your goals, and the particular students. Collecting too much information is as problematic as not collecting enough.

- "Front-load" instruction. This simply means that you should be clear about the goals of instruction and make those explicit to the students. For example, if students are going to read about environmental issues and be asked to take a position, they will need to learn how to distinguish fact from opinion, synthesize information, and draw conclusions. Both you and the students have a better chance of achieving your goals if you make clear to them the relationship between the skills they are learning and the task they are completing.

- Help students understand what good reading and writing look like by providing them with examples, examining work together, and discussing criteria. For example, help the class develop criteria for a good research report or book talk and then have children evaluate their work according to the criteria. Use criteria and scoring rubrics provided with instructional materials with the children instead of using them just for grading.

- Make self-assessment a dependable, integral part of your classroom. Begin with non-academic activities such as judging how well the class is working in groups, or how sharing time is working, or discussing favorite artwork. Some of these activities require students to consider qualities of good performance; others require judgments based on personal criteria. Both, however, require students to step back from their work or their behavior to think reflectively about it. You will need to develop these abilities over time with your students.

■ When assessing growth over time, be sure to consider both the assessment task and the individual student. For example, if you want to assess students' ability to read and summarize, the difficulty of the text and the type of text will be important to consider. A student's summary of a second-grade text at the beginning of the year may be better than his summary of a fifth-grade text at the end of the year, but the change in difficulty level would signal growth. Similarly, the topic or text type (narrative vs. information) will influence the quality of students' summaries. Multiple measures are especially important when assessing growth.

■ Create a system to help you keep track of the assessment information. Some teachers use a three-ring notebook with a section for each student, others use a computerized system, and others use a combination of work folders/ portfolios and teacher records. Whatever system you use, be sure to keep samples of student work and to document your assessments. These samples will help you communicate with both parents and students, providing the evidentiary trail of students' learning. If collections of work are set up collaboratively with students, they provide an excellent vehicle for conversation about students' strengths, needs, and future goals. In addition, by looking across students' folders, you will be able to analyze your instruction. It will become obvious, for example, the kinds of activities on which students are spending most of their time and areas in which they need more support.

■ Use classroom assessments to help with grading. You do not need to grade every piece of work or every assessment. The evidence you collect will provide the basis for the grades you assign. Some of the more formal assessments such as tests, performance activities, and projects are easier to grade. Other assessments such as oral discussions, response journals and rough drafts of writing are more difficult to grade but still provide useful information. Together, these graded and ungraded artifacts provide strong evidence for your grading decisions.

■ Begin classroom assessment slowly. Make good use of assessments that come with your instructional program or assessments you already have in place. You don't need to develop everything from scratch. Begin with several important outcomes, take time to review assessment results, and then use those results to shape your instruction. Classroom assessment is the piece of the puzzle that will most influence your teaching and student achievement. It takes time, but it is time well spent.

Final Thoughts

The goal of assessment is to improve learning and teaching. In truth, we cannot be good teachers nor can students be effective learners unless we use evidence to guide instruction and learning. By understanding the different types of assessments and using them wisely, we are more likely to make those good decisions. When the pieces of the puzzle are fit together, they provide a clear picture of learning and a road map to success. ■

Author

Sheila W. Valencia is Professor of Curriculum and Instruction at the University of Washington, Seattle where she conducts research and teaches in the area of Language, Literacy, and Culture. A nationally recognized expert in the field of literacy assessment and professional development, Dr. Valencia has published widely in journals such as *Reading Research Quarterly, Journal of Literacy Research, The Reading Teacher,* and *Language Arts*. She is author of *Literacy Portfolios in Action* and contributing author to *Houghton Mifflin Reading: A Legacy of Literacy*.

"Words, so innocent and powerless as they are, standing in a dictionary; how potent for good and evil they become in the hands of one who knows how to choose and combine them."

— Nathaniel Hawthorne

Teaching and Developing Vocabulary: Key to Long-Term Reading Success

John J. Pikulski and Shane Templeton

The Central Importance of Vocabulary

Perhaps the greatest tools we can give students for succeeding, not only in their education but more generally in life, is a large, rich vocabulary and the skills for using those words. Our ability to function in today's complex social and economic worlds is mightily affected by our language skills and word knowledge.

In addition to the vital importance of vocabulary for success in life, a large vocabulary is more specifically predictive and reflective of high levels of reading achievement. **The Report of the National Reading Panel (2000), for example, concluded, "The importance of vocabulary knowledge has long been recognized in the development of reading skills. As early as 1924, researchers noted that growth in reading power relies on continuous growth in word knowledge"** (pp. 4–15).

Vocabulary or Vocabularies?

In everyday conversation we speak of vocabulary in the singular; we speak of a person's vocabulary. This is actually an oversimplification. The American Heritage Dictionary defines vocabulary as "the sum of words used by, understood by, or at the command of a particular person or group." In this paper we are concerned with extending the sum of words that are used by and understood by students.

However, it seems important to point out that in almost all cases there are some differences in the number of words that an individual understands and uses. Even the terms "uses" and "understands" need clarification. For example, the major way in which we "use" vocabulary is when we speak and write; the term expressive vocabulary is used to refer to both since these are the vocabularies we use to express ourselves. We "understand" vocabulary when we listen to speech and when we read; the term receptive vocabulary is used to refer to listening and reading

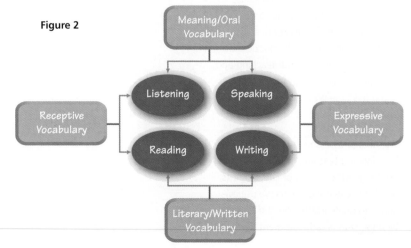

Figure 2

vocabularies. Finally, to round out the terminology, meaning or oral vocabulary refers to the combination of listening and speaking vocabularies, and literate vocabulary refers to the combination of our reading and writing vocabularies. Are our listening, speaking, reading,

> **… written language is more formal, more complex, and more sophisticated than spoken language.**

and writing vocabularies all the same? Are they equally large? Is our meaning vocabulary larger or smaller than our literate vocabularies? Figure 2 shows the relationship of the eight different terms.

For the first five years or so of their lives, children are involved in the process of acquiring a meaning/oral vocabulary—words that they understand when they hear them and that they can use in their speech. During this period, children have essentially no literate vocabularies. Most children acquire reading and writing skills upon entering school. They need to acquire a basic knowledge of how printed letters relate to the sounds of spoken words and how printed words relate to spoken words. Being able to translate or transcode print into speech allows children to use what they know about meaning/oral vocabulary for their literate vocabulary. So for very young children, their meaning vocabularies are much larger than their literate vocabularies.

The acquisition of decoding skills leads to rapid expansion of literate vocabularies by allowing children to transcode their meaning vocabularies into their literate vocabularies. This is so much the case that for older students and for adults our literate vocabularies are probably larger than our meaning vocabularies. We tend to have a larger group of words that we use in reading and writing than we use in our own speech. This is because written language is more formal, more complex, and more sophisticated than spoken language.

High-frequency vocabulary refers to those words that are used over and over again in our communications—they are important to both our meaning and literate vocabularies. A mere 100 words make up about 50% of most English texts; 200 words make up 90% of the running words of materials through third grade; and 500 words make up 90% of the running words in materials through ninth grade. If a reader is to have at least a modicum of fluency, it is critical that these words be taught systematically and effectively.

The research of Ehri (1994, 1998) is particularly informative. Her research strongly suggests that high-frequency words should be introduced without written context so that students focus on their visual composition, that they should be practiced in materials that are at an appropriate level of challenge, and that they should be practiced several times in order to allow developing readers to recognize them instantly or, in other words, at sight. She also makes the important point that although many of these words do not conform completely to phonic generalizations or expectations (e.g. *was*), they nonetheless very fre-

quently do have elements that are regular. For example, the *w* in *was* is regular and the *s* at the end of that word sometimes does have the /z/ sound. Ehri's research strongly suggests that these phonic regularities are powerful mnemonics for remembering the words and should be pointed out, rather than expecting that students will remember the vague shape of the word, as was the tradition with flash-card instruction for many years.

The Need to Improve Vocabulary Instruction

While the dependence of both general achievement and reading achievement on vocabulary growth has been clearly established for decades, those findings do not appear to have been put into practice. In a recent text, Beck et al. (2002) draw the research-based conclusion: "All the available evidence indicates that there is little emphasis on the acquisition of vocabulary in school curricula." In a classic classroom observational study, Durkin (1979) found that in the 4,469 minutes of reading instruction that were observed, a mere 19 minutes were devoted to vocabulary instruction and that virtually no vocabulary development instruction took place during content instruction such as social studies.

The effects of the lack of attention to vocabulary instruction, however, may not manifest themselves in the earliest grades where tests of reading achievement tend to contain passages that have simple content and common vocabulary. While most students who succeed in reading in the early grades continue to achieve well, some do not. The Report of the Rand Reading Study Group (2002) concluded, "Research has shown that many children who read at

Additional Resources

not the result of decoding problems or inability to comprehend narrative texts. Instead, it seems to be due to weakness in ability to comprehend informational texts (Progress in International Reading Literacy Study, 2003). When compared to students from the 35 participating nations, United States fourth graders ranked fourth on the narrative section of the test but thirteenth on the informational section. This disparity of nine rankings was by far the largest among the nations participating in the study.

A Comprehensive Approach to Teaching and Developing Vocabulary

The amount of vocabulary that children need to acquire each year is staggering in scope, estimated to be about 3,000 words a year. Therefore, a comprehensive approach consisting of the following components needs to be in place.

- Use "instructional" read-aloud events.

- Provide direct instruction in the meanings of clusters of words and individual words.

- Systematically teach students the meaning of prefixes, suffixes, and root words.

- Link spelling instruction to reading and vocabulary instruction.

- Teach the effective, efficient, realistic use of dictionaries, thesauruses, and other reference works.

- Teach, model, and encourage the application of a word-learning strategy.

- Encourage wide reading.

- Create a keen awareness of and a deep interest in language and words.

the third grade level in grade 3 will not automatically become proficient comprehenders in later grades."

Indeed, a commonly reported phenomenon in reading test results is for achievement to be good through second or third grade and to falter thereafter. This drop off in achievement seems very likely due to weaknesses in language development and background knowledge, which are increasingly required for reading comprehension beyond the early grades and for reading informational and content-area texts.

The most recently released study of international reading achievement provides some strong evidence that the weakness in U.S. student performance is

Use Instructional Read-Aloud Events

The recommendation that parents and teachers read aloud to children is among the most popular recommendations in the field of reading. The prestigious research-based report Becoming a Nation of Readers (Anderson et al. 1985) concluded, "The single most important activity for building the knowledge required for eventual success in reading is reading aloud to children." One very obvious way in which reading aloud to children can be expected to be beneficial is to increase their language and vocabulary skills. Indeed there is research to support this position (Elley, 1989; Leong and Pikulski, 1990; Robbins and Ehri, 1994).

The study by Elley (1989) strongly suggested that vocabulary growth was much greater when teachers discussed, even if briefly, the meanings of the words in addition to just reading the books aloud. The recent study by Juel et al. (2003) showed that while teachers in kindergarten and first grade spent considerable time reading and discussing books to children with below average vocabularies, these activities had minimal impact on the progress of the children. Only when teachers spent focused time on the vocabulary did significant growth occur. We apply the term "instructional read aloud" to read-aloud events where, in addition to reading aloud to stimulate an interest in books and reading, there is also a deliberate teaching of skills that will promote independence in reading, such as an increased vocabulary.

Provide Direct Instruction in the Meanings of Words

Which words should be taught? In deciding which words to teach we have found it helpful to think about "levels" of vocabulary, which is similar to what Beck et al. (2002) refer to as "tiers" of vocabulary.

Level I Words These are words that are used over and over in everyday speech. Since they are so frequently used in a variety of contexts, virtually all children

learn them. Some examples of these words would be *house, girl, cat, up, umbrella,* etc. Level I words are sometimes referred to as "conversational speech." Children who are learning English as a second language will sometimes make progress with this level of vocabulary but have difficulty making progress with words at levels beyond this one.

Level II Words These are words that are likely to be learned only through reading or through instruction. They have been referred to as the vocabulary of educated persons, as "academic vocabulary," and as "instructional vocabulary." They are words that are necessary for general success in school.

Words such as *perspective, generate, initiate, intermediate, calculation,* etc. are possible examples.

Level III Words These are words associated with a particular field of study or profession. These words make up the technical vocabulary or jargon of a field. Examples of Level III words from the field of reading instruction include the terms *digraph, diphthong, schwa, meta-comprehension,* etc. As one might expect, some words such as calculation might be classified as either a Level II or Level III word or both.

Level IV Words These are words that are interesting but so rare and esoteric that they are probably not useful even in most educational environments, and they are not associated with a field of study or profession. Examples are words that were but no longer are used: *majuscule* (a capital letter), *xanthodont* (one who has yellow teeth like a rodent), *noctuary* (an account of what happens in a night). Notice, however, that some Level IV words are useful for teaching morphological clues such as *noct* meaning "night" and *dont* or *dent* referring to teeth. Level IV words are also helpful for creating an interest in words and language.

Just by their definitions, it should be apparent that a major responsibility of teachers is to expand the Level II and Level III words of their students. Teachers of content areas have a special responsibility for teaching Level III words.

Systematically Teach the Meaning of Prefixes, Suffixes, and Root Words

The majority of English words have been created through the combination of morphemic elements, that is, prefixes and suffixes with base words and word roots. If learners understand

Additional Resources

how this combinatorial process works, they possess one of the most powerful understandings necessary for vocabulary growth (Anderson and Freebody, 1981). This understanding of how meaningful elements combine is defined as morphological knowledge because it is based on an understanding of morphemes, the smallest units of meaning in a language. In the intermediate grades and beyond, most new words that students encounter in their reading are morphological derivatives of familiar words (Aronoff, 1994). In recent years research has suggested some promising guidelines for teaching the meanings of prefixes, suffixes, and word roots as well as for the ways in which knowledge of these meaningful word parts may be applied (Templeton, 2004). Word roots such as *dict, spect,* and *struct* are meaningful parts of words that remain after all prefixes and suffixes have been removed but that usually do not stand by themselves as words: *prediction, inspection, contract.*

In the primary grades students begin to explore the effects of prefixes such as *un-, re-,* and *dis-* on base words. In the intermediate grades students continue to explore prefixes and an increasing number of suffixes and their effects on base words: *govern* (verb) + *-ment* = *government* (noun). Common Greek and Latin roots begin to be explored, along with the effects of prefixes and suffixes that attach to them (Templeton, 1989). These include, for example, *chron* ("time," as in *chron*ology), *tele* ("distant, far" as in *tele*vision), and *fract* ("break," as in *fract*ure). A large proportion of the vocabulary of specific content areas is built on Greek and Latin elements. As this morphological knowledge develops, teachers can model how it may be applied to determining the

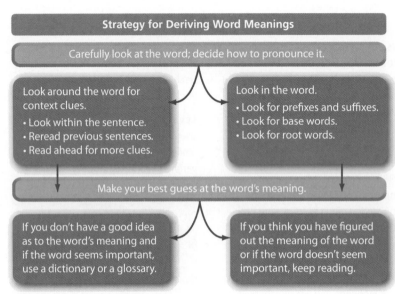

Figure 3

meanings of unfamiliar words encountered in print.

Link Spelling Instruction to Reading and Vocabulary Instruction

Spelling knowledge applies not only to the ability to encode words during writing; importantly, it also underlies individuals' ability to decode words during the process of reading (Templeton, 2003a, 2003b). Students' spelling knowledge is, therefore, a powerful foundation for their reading and their vocabulary development. This latter aspect is linked to the role that morphological knowledge plays, as discussed in the previous section. Words that are related in meaning are often related in spelling, despite changes in sound.

Among intermediate students, examination of how spelling patterns reflect meaning leads to vocabulary growth. To get a sense of how the connection works between spelling and meaning, examine the following words: *bomb/ bombard; muscle/muscular; compete/ competition.* Because the words in each pair are related in meaning, the spelling of the underlined sounds remains con-

stant; although the sound that letters represent may change in related words, the spelling usually remains the same because it preserves the meaning relationship that these words share.

Once students understand the spelling-meaning relationships among words, they can learn how the spelling or structure of familiar words can be clues to the spelling and the meaning of unknown words, and vice-versa. For example, a student who spells *condemn* as *condem* in her spontaneous writing may be shown the word *condemnation:* This not only explains the so-called "silent" *n* in *condemn* but expands the student's vocabulary at the same time.

Teach the Use of Dictionaries, Thesauruses, and Other Reference Works

Exploring dictionary entries can be one important and effective component of understanding a word deeply. The entries can also help students determine the precise meaning of a word.

Dictionaries can also provide helpful information about the history of a word and reinforce the interrelationships among words in the same meaning "families." For example, a discussion of run-on entries illustrates how one word's entry can include information about related words—the entry for entrap also includes entraps and entrapment. The usage notes in dictionaries often explain subtle but important differences among words—usually the appropriateness of one word over

another in a particular context. Words for which the dictionary is essential may be entered in a student's vocabulary notebook. Dictionaries can also contribute to an interest in and attitudes toward words that teachers and students explore.

Teach the Application of a Word Learning Strategy

As noted earlier, written texts contain richer vocabulary and, therefore, more opportunities for expansion of vocabulary through reading as compared to the word challenge in oral language. However, the probability of learning a new word's meaning through encoun-

tering it in reading is not high—only about one chance in 20. There is research that shows that students can be taught strategic behaviors to improve their ability to learn the meaning of words (Kuhn and Stahl, 1998). While skills such as application of morphological clues, reference works, and spelling clues to word meanings are all useful, they become more powerful and func-

tional when combined with the use of context clues in a deliberate strategy.

Based on a review of research and our experience in working with students, we suggest the following sequence:

Step 1: Carefully look at the word; decide how to pronounce it. Carefully processing the letters or chunks of letters of a word and thinking about the sounds for them will leave a memory trace for the word even if it is not a word that the reader knows. At very least, it is likely that if the reader encounters the word again in future readings, there will be at least a modicum of familiarity with it.

Step 2a: Look around the word for context clues, including:

- Look within the sentence.
- Reread previous sentences.
- Read ahead for more context clues.

Step 2b: Look in the word for prefixes and suffixes, base words, and root words that might offer clues. We have listed this and the previous step as 2a and 2b because with experience students will apply one or the other first depending on the word. For a word with a common prefix such as *un-*, morphological clues would likely be used before the use of context clues. The hallmark of a strategic reader is the flexible application of strategies.

Step 3: Make your best guess at the word's meaning. It is important to stress with students that natural context most often will not lead to a clear understanding of a word's meaning and that some words will not contain recognizable morphological clues. Nevertheless, it seems useful to take the step of making a best guess at the word's meaning since this further mental activity is likely to make the word more familiar the next time it is encountered—even if the student's understanding of the word has to be revised.

Step 4a: If you don't have a good idea as to the word's meaning and if the word seems important, use a dictionary or glossary. We suggest two touchstones for determining whether or not a word is important. First, if the reader is beginning to have difficulty understanding what he or she is reading, the meaning of the word may contribute to a better understanding of what is being read. It is, therefore, important. Second, if it is a word that the reader has encountered before and still has no good idea as to its meaning, it is probably an important word since it is likely to be encountered again in the future.

Step 4b: If you think you have figured out the meaning of the word or if the word doesn't seem important, keep reading. It would be unrealistic to tell a reader to look up every unknown word in a dictionary; mature readers don't. Therefore, it is legitimate to move on and keep reading if context and morphological clues have been somewhat helpful or if the word doesn't seem to be important for comprehension of what is being read or for adding to one's functional vocabulary.

Teachers need to strategically and flexibly model and teach each of the above steps. Eventually, as students mature in their reading skills, they can and will internalize the steps in this strategy. Application of these steps then becomes much smoother and more automatic, requiring less attention. In fact, good readers usually "blend" these steps.

Encourage Wide Reading

The importance of wide reading in the growth of students' vocabulary is critical (Nagy and Anderson, 1984). Given the staggering number of new words that children must add to their vocabularies each year, it would be impossible to directly teach all of them; Anderson (1996) estimates that it would require teaching about 20 new words a day each day of the school year!

Through wide independent reading, students come in contact with vocabulary that rarely occurs in spoken language but that is much more likely to be encountered in printed language. Cunningham and Stanovich (1998) present evidence that vocabulary used in oral communication such as television shows or adult conversation is extremely restricted. For example, prime time television shows have less challenging vocabulary than children's books, and college graduates talking with friends and spouses use vocabulary that is less challenging than that in preschool books!

Conclusions

It does seem hard to overstate the importance of vocabulary—not only for reading achievement but also for general social and economic success. The early years of a child's life have a profound influence on that child's language and vocabulary development, which in turn greatly influences school success. Children who live in poverty in their early years have much less verbal interaction with their parents and consequently begin school with far less vocabulary development than their more privileged peers. While the language gap doesn't widen once children from lower socioeconomic backgrounds enter the stimulating environment of school, that gap does not narrow. Research suggests that it may not narrow because the vocabulary instruction offered is not sufficiently intense or effective.

Research is clear regarding implications for instruction that will ensure the development of large, useful vocabularies: wide reading plays a critical role in developing knowledge, and teachers facilitate this process by teaching strategies for learning words independently, including teaching morphological units, the use of dictionaries and other reference works, and exploring the link between spelling and learning words. Teachers should also directly teach important specific words, and they should develop and sustain students' interest in and curiosity about words. ■

Authors

John J. Pikulski is Professor of Education at the University of Delaware, where he has been Director of the Reading Center, Department Chairperson, and President of the University Faculty Senate. He has served as a reading and psychological consultant to numerous school districts and reading and governmental agencies throughout North America. His current research interests focus on strategies for preventing reading problems and the teaching and developing of vocabulary. An active member in the International Reading Association, Dr. Pikulski has served on its Board of Directors, chaired various committees, contributed a monthly column to its journal, and was president of the association in 1997–98. He is the coauthor of *The Diagnosis, Correction, and Prevention of Reading Disabilities* and *Informal Reading Inventories*, and has been inducted into the prestigious Reading Hall of Fame.

Shane Templeton is Foundation Professor of Curriculum and Instruction at the University of Nevada, Reno. Dr. Templeton's research has focused on developmental word knowledge in elementary, middle, and high school students. His books include *Children's Literacy: Contexts for Meaningful Learning* and *Teaching the Integrated Language Arts*. He is coauthor of *Words Their Way: Word Study for Phonics, Vocabulary, and Spelling Instruction*.

Dr. Templeton is the senior author of *Houghton Mifflin Spelling and Vocabulary* and an author of *Houghton Mifflin English* and *Houghton Mifflin Reading*. Since 1987, Dr. Templeton has been a member of the Usage Panel of *The American Heritage Dictionary*.

Ehri's Four Stages of Reading Development

Pre-Alphabetic Stage of Development

The reader has no appreciation of the alphabetic principle and attempts to use visual clues in the printed word to identify the word.

▼

Partial Alphabetic Stage of Development

While recognizing a relationship between letters and sounds, the reader may only focus on specific easily identifiable parts of the word.

▼

Fully Alphabetic Stage of Development

Recognizing that sounds correspond to letters, readers are able to blend sounds to arrive at a pronunciation. Eventually these words are memorized as a unit and known by sight.

▼

Consolidated Alphabetic Stage of Development

Repeated encounters with words allow the reader to store letter patterns across different words.

Fluency: The Bridge from Decoding to Reading Comprehension

John J. Pikulski and David J. Chard

Introduction

Fluency, which has been referred to as a "neglected" and "ignored" aspect of reading (National Reading Panel, 2000), is receiving substantial attention at this time from both researchers and practitioners. This attention may stem, at least in part, from the fact that the highly influential Report of the National Reading Panel discusses fluency as one of only five critical components of the reading process.

Definitions of Reading Fluency

The National Reading Panel report defines reading fluency as "…the ability to read text quickly, accurately, and with proper expression" (p. 3–5). All three dimensions appear critical to a full definition of reading fluency (Dowhower, 1991). The fact that two of the three dimensions of fluency, accuracy, and expressiveness, can be observed only limited the amount of attention that fluency received until recently. Fluency was seen essentially as a word recognition and oral reading phenomenon, and the importance of oral reading pales dramatically in comparison to that of silent reading comprehension. Except, perhaps, as beginning readers in school, we spend a miniscule amount of time doing expressive oral reading as compared to silent reading comprehension.

The Literacy Dictionary: The Vocabulary of Reading and Writing, on the other hand, defines fluency as "freedom from word identification problems that might hinder comprehension" (Harris and Hodges, 1995, p. 85). Samuels, a pioneer in research and theory in reading fluency, cites the alteration and enlargement of the construct of fluency to include reading comprehension as a major force in elevating the importance of the construct in the field of reading. He notes, "To experience good reading comprehension, the reader must be able to identify words quickly and easily" (Samuels, 2002, p. 167).

The correlation between fluency and reading comprehension was clearly established by a large-scale analysis of data from the National Assessment of Educational Progress in Reading (Pinnell et al., 1995). In that study, 44 percent of the subjects were found to be disfluent when reading grade-level appropriate materials that they had previously read silently; the study also showed a significant, positive relationship between oral reading fluency and reading comprehension performance.

A comprehensive definition then would seem to relate the centrality of fluency to reading comprehension and the established dimensions of the construct. We would

Additional Resources

propose the following definition: Reading fluency refers to rapid, efficient, accurate word recognition skills that permit a reader to construct the meaning of text. Fluency is also manifested in accurate, rapid, expressive oral reading and is applied during, and makes possible, silent reading comprehension.

Ehri's Stages of Reading Development as They Relate to Fluency

In line with the theory of automaticity and the definition of fluency we have proposed, Ehri (1998) has noted, "Being able to read words by sight automatically is the key to skilled reading of text. This allows readers to process words in text quickly, without attention directed

> ### Improve reading fluency through:
>
> - Modeled reading
> - Repeated reading of familiar text
> - Wide independent reading
> - Coached reading of appropriately selected materials
> - Chunking of text
> - Word reading practice

to the word itself" (p. 11). Ehri has developed a carefully researched, elegant theory of how readers systematically progress in stages from being non-readers to the point where they can recognize words effortlessly.

Building Fluency in Developing Readers

Our perception is that until very recently many educators took a rather simplistic

approach to developing fluency which is summed up in the deceptively simple admonition: "Read, read, and read some more." The expectation was that if students read more, they would achieve fluency. However, Ehri's research and theories suggest that at least some students will need expert teacher guidance in order to progress efficiently through stages of reading development to fluency. Students who lack the necessary foundations for developing decoding skills are in no position to read, read, and read some more. Students who engage in reading, but who employ the guessing strategies of the Partial Alphabetic reader, are not likely to make optimal progress in reading.

Fortunately, several research studies have focused on the details of instruction that seem most promising for improving reading fluency. These instructional practices include: modeled reading, repeated reading of familiar text, wide independent reading, coached reading of appropriately selected materials, chunking of text, and word reading practice.

Modeled Reading

One way to enhance fluency is for teachers to read aloud to students (Dowhower, 1987; Hoffman, 1987; Smith, 1979). The process of reading aloud to students needs to be supplemented with procedures which actually engage students in interaction with text, but reading aloud does provide them with a model of how to pace reading in connected text and how to infuse expression (attend to dialogue marks and punctuation). Taped or computer modeled reading is also a viable way to provide fluency support. However, for younger and less able readers taped or computer modeled reading seems more

effective than no model, but not as effective as a teacher model (Daly and Martens, 1994). For lower performing readers, an additional benefit of having text read initially by a model improved comprehension. It seems that the reading model allowed students to focus on the content of the passage initially before they read it independently (Monda, 1989). While it varies from study to study whether students followed along in copies of the texts, we recommend this as a way to engage children in the text prior to their reading it independently.

Repeated Reading of Familiar Text

Rereading text or repeated oral reading is perhaps the most frequently documented approach to improving fluency (National Reading Panel, 2000; Rashotte and Torgesen, 1985) and has been associated with improved outcomes for young students (O'Shea, Sindelar, and O'Shea, 1987) as well as college students (Carver and Hoffman, 1981). Generally, intervention research on fluency development has been dominated by research on repeated reading. This likely reflects the application of the theory that fluent reading is promoted by frequent opportunities to practice in familiar text and to increased exposure to words.

Wide Independent Reading

Research does not yet clearly indicate whether repeated reading is superior to wide, sustained reading of different texts. Currently, it seems that for more able readers, repeated reading of the same texts is not as necessary as it is for struggling readers and that increasing the amount of reading that is done is sufficiently, and perhaps more, beneficial (Homan, Klesius, and Hite, 1993;

Mathes and Fuchs, 1993; Rashotte and Torgesen, 1985).

Previous highly respected research syntheses have been far less restrained about the salutary effects of wide reading. For example, Becoming a Nation of Readers (Anderson et al, 1985) concludes: "Research suggests that the amount of independent, silent reading that children do in school is significantly related to gains in reading achievement" (p. 76). This same research review concludes: "Research also shows that the amount of reading students do out of school is consistently related to gains in reading achievement" (p. 77). In her critical review of beginning reading research Adams (1990) concluded: "If we want children to read well, we must find a way to induce them to read lots" (p. 5). Adams also concludes: "Children should be given as much opportunity and encouragement as possible to practice their reading. Beyond the basics, chil-

dren's reading facility, as well as their vocabulary and conceptual growth, depends strongly on the amount of text they read" (p. 127).

Keith Stanovich and his colleagues (Cunningham and Stanovich, 1998; Nathan and Stanovich, 1991; Stanovich, 1986; Stanovich and Cunningham, 1992; Stanovich, Cunningham, and Freeman, 1984; Stanovich and West, 1989) have presented impressive research results and theoretical argument for the value of wide reading. The evidence and rationale that they present, however, is that the positive relationship between reading achievement and wide reading may not be affected exclusively through the development of fluency, but through the development of language and cognitive abilities as well.

While the experimental evidence may not be as clear as it should be, there does appear, at least for achieving readers, strong evidence and support for the

conclusion of Nathan and Stanovich (1991) that: "If children are to become fluent readers, they need to read a lot. Our job as educators is to see to it that children want to read—that they seek new knowledge via the written word and derive satisfaction and joy from the reading process" (p.179).

Moreover, if students are making adequate progress with fluency, wide reading rather than repeated reading may lead to greater improvements in vocabulary and comprehension. However, for less able readers experiencing particular difficulties with fluency, repeated reading remains an important aspect of an instructional program.

Coached or Assisted Reading

Most researchers agree that accuracy alone is insufficient and that students need to read rapidly if they are going to understand the connections that need to be made between ideas in print (Nathan and Stanovich, 1991). Controlling the difficulty of texts and providing feedback for words missed during reading seem to be associated with improved rate and accuracy for those students developing fluent reading. Advancing students through progressively difficult text based on their performance seems to enhance their overall fluency as does correction and feedback for words read incorrectly.

Providing students with opportunities to read widely and targeting specific elements of fluency building, such as progressively difficult text with corrective feedback, appear to contribute to improved fluency (Kuhn and Stahl, 2000). Heibert and Fisher (2002) studied fluency development as it relates to the features of the texts used for promoting fluency. Specifically, they were interested in examining the effects of texts in

Essential dimensions for the assessment of fluency include measures of:

1. Oral reading accuracy
2. Oral reading rate
3. Quality of oral reading
4. Reading comprehension

which particular text dimensions or features were carefully controlled. The treatment texts Heibert and Fisher designed were characterized as having the following key features: a small number of unique words, a high percentage of most frequently used words, and often repeated critical words (those words that influence the meaning of the text most). Students in the comparison group read from texts typically associated with commercial reading programs. Using a repeated reading (three times) instructional routine in a nine-week intervention, students reading in the treatment texts made significant gains in fluency over their peers in the comparison condition. There also seemed to be an effect for comprehension for second language learners. These findings suggest that the features of the texts being used to promote fluency should be carefully considered.

Chunking Texts

Another approach to fluency building is to provide struggling readers with text in which meaningful groups or words or phrases are signaled for the reader as a means of improving fluency and comprehension (Cromer, 1970; Young and Bowers, 1995). Research reveals that different amounts of text presented in repeated reading do not seem to

change the outcome. However, control of the amount of text presented may be beneficial for students who are experiencing difficulty with reading accuracy as it may force them to focus on the words for a longer period of time (Cohen, 1988).

Carbo (1981) used a phrased or chunked approach to assist repeated reading. She had students listen to tapes and follow along in books in which the text was chunked into short phrases. Carbo reported significant gains in word recognition ability suggesting that this approach might be helpful for improving accuracy.

Several researchers have studied the effects of parsing or chunking texts into phrase units. While most of these studies have been with older students, Kuhn and Stahl (2000) reported that reading phrase units rather than conventional text does seem to result in improved fluency.

Word Reading Practice

The importance of individual word reading automaticity would seem to have practical implications for fluency building. Studies in which teachers had students practice reading lists of words that they were to later encounter in connected texts consistently resulted in increased fluency (Fleisher, Jenkins, and Pany, 1979–80; Levy, Abello, and Lysynchuk, 1997).

It is important to note, however, that there was no concomitant increase in comprehension.

The Assessment of Fluency

As noted at the beginning of this paper, fluency has been referred to as the "neglected aspect" of reading. The assessment of fluency, in particular,

appears to have received very limited attention.

Based on the limited research on the assessment of fluency, and the construct and definition of fluency adopted in this paper, there seem to be several essential dimensions for the assessment of fluency, including measures of:

1) oral reading accuracy;
2) oral reading rate;
3) quality of oral reading; and
4) reading comprehension.

While all four of these dimensions can be evaluated informally as pointed out by the National Reading Panel, it would seem prudent to develop a fluency measure that addresses at least some traditional reliability and validity criteria. One comprehensive instrument that attempts to address all the essential dimensions of fluency and which has been subjected to extensive field-test trials is the Leveled Reading Passages (LRP) Assessment Kit (Houghton Mifflin). This instrument provides the materials and descriptions of procedures that allows for the assessment of a full construct of fluency for students who are at the very beginning stages of reading through sixth grade. The LRP was field tested in a study of 1,200 students across the United States. The field tests validated the decodability and the level of difficulty of the reading passages and word lists that are part of the instrument. Field-test data were also used to establish benchmarks of below-level, on-level, and above-level performance for oral reading accuracy, oral reading rate, quality of oral reading, and reading comprehension. Thus, the LRP addresses all the essential dimensions of fluency, capitalizes on the established strengths of informal assessment, but then uses actual field-test data to address the validity of the instrument.

Conclusions

While the construct of fluency may have been neglected in the past, it is receiving much deserved attention presently. There is a very strong research and theoretical base that indicates that while fluency in and of itself is not sufficient to ensure high levels of reading achievement and comprehension, fluency is absolutely necessary for that achievement and for comprehension. While fluency is most obviously reflected in oral reading, it more importantly operates in silent reading as well. If a reader has not developed fluency, the process of decoding words drains attention, and insufficient attention is available for constructing the meaning of texts. Fluency builds on a foundation of oral language skills, phonemic awareness, familiarity with letter forms, and efficient decoding skills. Ehri's description of the stages of word recognition explains how readers come to recognize words by sight through carefully processing print.

While more research is needed on issues of adequate rates of fluency at various grade levels and for judging the quality of oral reading, there is good agreement that the comprehensive assessment of fluency must include measures of oral reading accuracy, rate of oral reading, and quality of oral reading. There is also good agreement that these dimensions of fluency must be assessed within the context of reading comprehension. Fluency without accompanying high levels of reading comprehension is simply not adequate. ■

Authors

Dr. John J. Pikulski is Professor of Education at the University of Delaware, where he has been Director of the Reading Center, Department Chairperson, and President of the University Faculty Senate. His current research interests focus on strategies for preventing reading problems and the teaching and developing of vocabulary. An active member in the International Reading Association, Dr. Pikulski has served on its Board of Directors, chaired various committees, and was president of the association in 1997–98. He is coauthor of *The Diagnosis, Correction, and Prevention of Reading Disabilities* and *Informal Reading Inventories*. Dr. Pikulski is also a senior author of *Houghton Mifflin Reading*, and is a coordinating author on *Reading Intervention for EARLY SUCCESS™*.

Dr. David J. Chard is Associate Professor at the University of Oregon where he also serves as Director of Graduate Studies in Special Education. His research and teaching interests focus on early literacy and mathematics instruction for all students, including those with learning disabilities and those at risk for school failure. Currently, Dr. Chard is the principal investigator on two federal research projects on mathematics and reading comprehension instruction in the primary grades. He has published extensively on instruction interventions, improvement of teacher development programs, and word recognition processes in reading development. Dr. Chard is an author of *Houghton Mifflin Reading*, and is a consultant on *Houghton Mifflin Math*.

From Phonemic Awareness to Fluency: Effective Decoding Instruction in a Research-Based Reading Program

David J. Chard, John J. Pikulski, and Shane Templeton

Introduction

In today's society, it is absolutely critical that every child has the fullest opportunities to become an accomplished reader. Anyone unable to read and write proficiently faces enormous social, personal, and economic limitations in today's complex, information-flooded world. There is widespread agreement that the reading demands are greater now than at any previous time in history.

To function successfully, readers must be able to construct complex understandings, make critical comparisons, draw inventive conclusions, and carefully evaluate the materials they read. In addition, to fully capitalize on the power of reading, readers must also be able to appreciate the artistry of an accomplished author. Reading involves these multiple goals and much more. This view of reading as an active, dynamic, constructive, and critical process is the view reflected in recent reviews of reading research (e.g., National Research Council, 1998; National Reading Panel, 2000) and is the view of reading reflected in this paper.

One feature that distinguishes reading from other vehicles for acquiring, evaluating, applying, and appreciating information, such as listening to a lecture or witnessing a demonstration, is that reading depends on the ability to translate print into meaning. The first vitally important step in reading is being able to decode or recognize print. The process of being able to translate or transcode printed words into their spoken language equivalent has been variously labeled as word identification, word recognition, or decoding.

The *Literacy Dictionary* (Harris & Hodges, 1995) defines word recognition as "the process of determining the pronunciation and some degree of meaning of a word in written or printed form" (p. 283). Reading is sometimes seen as involving two major factors: word recognition that determines a word's pronunciation; and comprehension, or understanding its meaning.

Foundations for Learning to Decode: Understanding the Functions and Value of Reading

It is critically important that children learn to decode in the early grades. There is evidence that children who do not have a successful start in learning to read are not likely to catch up with their peers and become proficient readers (Frances,

Shaywitz, Stuebing, Shaywitz & Fletcher, 1996). What do children need in order to be successful in learning to read? Adams (1990), in her comprehensive review of the topic of learning to decode, concludes that ". . . the most important activity for building the knowledge and skills eventually required for reading is that of reading aloud to children" (p. 86). She goes on to elaborate:

> It is not just reading to children that makes the difference, it is enjoying the books with them and reflecting on their form and content. It is developing and supporting the children's curiosity about text and the meanings it conveys. It is encouraging the children to examine the print. And it is showing the children that we value and enjoy reading and that we hope they will too. (p. 87)

Adams estimates that preschool children who live in literacy-rich environments come to school having been read to for over 1,000 hours and that this figure may be double in some cases. She also points out, however, that preschool children from environments that provide few literacy experiences have been read to for 25 hours or less, and some not at all. She suggests that there is much that needs to be done to provide children with the fullest opportunities to learn to read:

> To this end, the great value of research on prereaders may lie in the clues it gives us toward determining what the less prepared prereader needs most to learn. For these children, we have not a classroom moment to waste.

> The evidence strongly suggests that we must help them to develop their awareness of the phonemic composition of words. And we must also teach them the letters of the alphabet and the phonemic significance of each. But what else? The 'reading-ready' child enters school with a substantial base of prereading skills and wealth of experience with and knowledge about the pleasures and functions of text and about literary language and styles. (p. 90)

Adams goes on to cite the importance of creating a literate classroom environment; of relating reading to work, play, and living; and of providing opportunities to see how reading provides needed

information. She concludes that just as we must provide for the physical and emotional needs of young children, "We must do as much with reading. In our society, their lives depend on it" (p. 107).

In the sections that follow we outline the importance of teaching and developing a number of more specific areas important for reading success. Those factors, however, should be considered in the broad context of ensuring that children have many opportunities to understand the functions, the benefits, and the joys of reading, and ensuring, as fully as possible, that they have many opportunities for developing confidence in their ability to learn to read.

Language Development

There is a clear and obvious link between the various aspects of language development. Listening, speaking, reading, and

Additional Resources

writing are all forms of language development, and as such are highly interrelated. Listening and speaking skills, oral forms of language, develop earlier and form a foundation for building reading and writing skills, written forms of language development. The word *home,* for example, raises a host of meanings, associations, and memories regardless of whether it is read or heard. As the National Research Council (1998) points out, **"Many basic cognitive processes are shared during reading and listening. Syntactic and inferential processes as well as background and word knowledge play a role in both"** **(p. 64).** The council goes on to cite studies that show that the correlations between listening comprehension and reading comprehension tend to be low in the early grades, but they rise through about sixth grade. The relationship between language development and reading achievement is lower in the early grades for several reasons. First, achievement in reading in the early grades is highly dependent on decoding skills, which are less directly related to language development. Second, most beginning reading materials minimize language and conceptual challenges in order to allow children to focus their energies and attention on word identification. Even beginning reading instruction, however, should include language expansion activities so that children build the language skills and background information they will need to read more complex reading materials as they progress through the grades.

Concepts of Print

The term concepts of print refers to children's knowledge of the conventions of printed English language, for example, that we read English from left to right and top to bottom. The term also describes familiarity with and the ability to use terms like *letter, word,* and *sentence* as applied to print. It also describes the insight that there is a correspondence between the number of printed words in a text and the number of spoken words that are read, and the ability to apply that insight while reading, often referred to as the ability to "track print." As the Learning First Alliance document (1998) indicates, "Children need to know that stories and other texts are written from left to right, and that there is a one-to-one correspondence between the words on a page and the words a reader says" (p. 11).

Letter Recognition

Letters are the building blocks of print. It seems only reasonable that learning to read depends completely on the ability to accurately and rapidly recognize the letters of the alphabet and to discriminate each letter from the others, sometimes referred to as orthographic familiarity. Indeed, there is massive research evidence to support this conclusion (Andersen, et al., 1985; Adams, 1990; Ehri, 1991; National Research Council, 1998). For example, Adams (1990) concludes, "There exists a wealth of evidence that the speed and accuracy with which young readers can recognize individual letters is a critical determinant of their reading proficiency and future growth" (p. 112).

Phonemic Awareness

Concepts of print and letter recognition deal with the visual dimensions of language; phonemic awareness deals with the oral dimensions of language. As explained in other parts of this paper, English is an alphabetic language, which means that a small number of graphemes represent the sounds of the oral forms of the language. In English there are approximately 42–44 different speech sounds. (Linguistic experts disagree on the exact number, and the number of different sounds varies from one English dialect to another.) The terms phonological and phonemic awareness refer to the insight that spoken language consists of identifiable units; for example, that utterances are composed of spoken words, that spoken words consist of one or more syllables, and that spoken words and syllables are composed of sounds.

Measures of phonemic awareness are among the best, if not the best, predictors of success in learning to read (Adams, 1990; National Research Council, 1998; Learning First Alliance, 1998; National Reading Panel, 2000). In the early stages of learning to read, children rely on "sounding out" words—associating printed letters with the sounds of oral language and blending these sounds together. If children have not developed the insight that oral words are composed of a limited number of units called sounds, they will not be able to use this fundamental approach to word identification. Being able to think about the sounds in spoken words (phonemic segmentation) is critically and directly related to spelling ability, and being able to blend sounds together to form oral words (phonemic blending) is critically important and directly related to acquiring reading skills. While the term phonological awareness refers to a variety of sound units in spoken language such as spoken word, syllable, onsets, and rimes, the critical units for reading appear to be phonemes, and the critical phonemic awareness skills appear to be blending and segmenting phonemes (National Reading Panel, 2000). (See

Pikulski & Templeton, 1998, for a fuller discussion of phonemic awareness.)

Phases of Development in Learning to Decode Words

The work of Linnea Ehri (for example, 1985, 1991, 1995) has been particularly informative in exploring the developmental process of learning to read words. Ehri has identified four developmental phases: pre-alphabetic, partial alphabetic, full alphabetic, and consolidated alphabetic.

> **A number of researchers … have demonstrated that reading words and spelling words are not separate, distinct processes but rather processes that draw upon the same types of underlying word knowledge.**

The pre-alphabetic phase characterizes how emergent readers "read" words. They do not make associations between letters and sounds because they have not yet gained insight into the alphabetic principle. Rather, they associate particular visual characteristics of words, and the context in which they occur, with a meaning. For example they may "read" the word *produce* in a supermarket as "fruit" or "veg-

gies;" they use context and meaning to generate a response to print, but their response lacks accuracy because they cannot yet make use of the alphabetic principle.

In the partial alphabetic phase children attend to at least some salient sounds within words; they make connections between some of the letters and sounds, usually at the beginning and endings of words. They are not yet systematically processing the letters in a word and aren't consciously attending to vowels. A child may learn to read the word *sun,* for example, by noticing the letters *s* and *n* and realizing that these letters correspond to the sounds she hears when she says the word. In this type of partial connection, *sn* stays in a child's memory and may help her to identify *sun* when she next sees it; however, since only partial information is used, words like *sign* and *soon* may also be misidentified as *sun.* Children at this stage need instruction and experiences that will help them move to the full alphabetic phase.

In the full alphabetic phase children can and do attend consciously to all of the sounds within a word. Because of this, they are able to form complete connections between the letters in the written word and the sounds in the spoken word. Most importantly, this ability allows them to 1) decode words they have not seen before because they now know the sounds that letters are most likely to represent and can reliably make use of those letter/sound associations, and 2) learn and remember sight words much more easily and effectively.

Through careful attention to print in sequential decoding, children begin to notice that the same patterns of letters, such as -*at* and -*ike* occur in

many words. Instruction that focuses on these patterns and the experience of reading these patterns over and over in words leads to the ability to process or "chunk" the letters as a single unit rather than as three separate letters. When readers are able to do this, they are in the consolidated alphabetic phase.

A word such as *shake,* for example, is now read as two units, *sh* and *ake,* whereas at the full alphabetic level it would be read as three parts, *sh* + *a* + *k.* This ability to read letter patterns as units allows the more rapid identification and processing of words during reading, making reading words a much more automatic process. This building of fluency, in turn, allows the reader to spend more time thinking about what is being read. Over time, readers' sight vocabularies include many polysyllabic words. Syllable patterns come to play a role in word recognition (Taft, 1991) as well as meaning or morphemic patterns (Derwing, Smith, & Wiebe, 1995; Fowler & Liberman, 1995; Templeton, 1992). More advanced readers, therefore, apply their knowledge of spelling and meaning patterns in recognizing words.

A number of researchers have emphasized the role of spelling in the development of word knowledge (Ehri, 1986, 1997; Frith, 1985; Henderson, 1990; Templeton & Bear, 1992; Treiman, 1993). They have demonstrated that reading words and spelling words are not separate, distinct processes but rather processes that draw upon the same types of underlying word knowledge. The type of alphabetic information that readers use to read words is the same type of information they use to spell words. For example, a child in the partial alphabetic phase whose

Additional Resources

1. Sequential decoding
2. Use of spelling patterns or analogy
3. Use of morphemic elements
4. Use of context clues
5. Automatic recognition
6. Strategically using combinations of the above

Beginning readers who are drawing upon full-alphabetic knowledge, through their knowledge of phonics and their ability to blend phonemes, are able to decode words sequentially, letter by letter, identifying the sound associated with each letter and then blending the sounds together. While this is a relatively time and energy-consuming way to identify words, it is reliable, and this careful processing of print allows the beginning reader to store letter patterns and eventually whole words that can be used to more efficiently and effectively decode words. As a result, beginning readers who carefully process print can move into the consolidated alphabetic stage of development and recognize common letter combinations or spelling patterns (*at, og,* etc.) as units.

Readers can also identify a word by analogy. If a part of the word looks like another word that they know, they can use that information to determine the identity of the unknown word. The unfamiliar word *snake* would be recognized as containing the pattern -*ake,* which also occurs in *cake,* a word that is known.

As students progress through the grades, they also increasingly use

morphology to decode words (Scott & Nagy, 1994; Smith, 1998; Sternberg & Powell, 1983; Wysocki & Jenkins, 1987). Morphemes, the smallest units of meaning in a language, can be individual words that have meaning on their own, such as *desk* and *run;* they can be word parts that change and extend the meaning of words to which they are added, such as prefixes (*un-, re-, dis-*) or suffixes (-*ful* and -*ity*); and they can be Greek or Latin word roots that usually do not stand alone as words but are the meaning "anchor" to which affixes attach, such as *chron* ("time," as in *chronology*) and *tract* ("draw or pull," as in *tractor* and *attract*). Like the use of spelling patterns and word patterns, the use of morphemes to identify words is efficient because the reader is responding to units larger than a single letter.

Beginning readers can sometimes use context to help identify an unknown word. Context includes the surrounding text as well as picture clues. However, there is substantial research showing that younger and poorer readers rely more on context than do skillful readers (Stanovich, 1980; Adams, 1990). If beginning readers rely heavily on context as a word identification strategy, they experience considerable difficulty in developing their sight-word vocabularies. Even when they correctly identify a word using context, they will most likely not know the word the next time they encounter it in print—they have no way of holding onto it in memory because they did not examine the connections between letters and sounds within the words. As Adams puts it, "To the extent that children use context to avoid fully processing and, thereby, learning about the spelling of words, it may in the long run slow their reading growth" (p. 178).

mental representation for the written word *sun* is *sn* is also likely to spell the word as *sn.* In fact, instruction in spelling is probably the best way for partial alphabetic readers to become fully phonemically aware. At this phase and at the full alphabetic phase, spelling can be a "pacemaker" for reading. In the process of spelling or writing, students extend their knowledge of the alphabetic system, and this knowledge informs the strategies they use to decode words during reading (Frith, 1985; Morris & Perney, 1984).

How Words Can Be Identified

Readers have several possibilities available for identifying written words:

On the other hand, contextual analysis is useful in that it can provide confirmation of an initial hypothesis about a word's identity. If readers understand how to decode a word using phonics, their knowledge of spelling patterns, syllable patterns, and/or morphemic elements, then context can provide a useful "check" or confirmation of the word. This check occurs, however, after the word has at least been tentatively identified using more reliable, effective strategies such as letter-by-letter sounding out of the word or use of word parts.

The best means of identifying words during reading is to retrieve them from memory, without conscious effort, as sight words. A primary goal for beginning reading, therefore, is to assist children in developing sight vocabularies. It is critical that the important goal of developing a large fund of sight words not be confused with the outdated, discredited sight approach to teaching words in which beginning readers were instructed to learn words as "wholes" without reference to letter-sound associations and spelling patterns. Instead, research shows that instruction can best be done through 1) helping children to examine the spellings of words, thinking about how the spellings symbolize sounds, and then blending the sounds, and 2) engaging them in reading texts in which they have opportunities to reinforce their developing sight vocabulary and apply word recognition strategies to unfamiliar words, which become part of their sight vocabularies.

Developing readers need to be taught to be flexible and strategic in their approach to identifying words. In the initial stages of learning to read, they will need to rely on sequential decoding, paying careful attention to the orderly relationship that exists between letters and sounds and monitoring their decoding attempts to ensure that what they are reading makes sense. As their experience with printed words and word parts grows, they will recognize clusters of letters and whole words, which will move them toward greater fluency; however, even fluent readers will sometimes need to revert to sequential decoding in order to decode an unfamiliar word.

Characteristics of Effective Phonics Instruction

Children benefit from organized instruction that centers on sounds, letters, the relationships between sounds and letters, and the application of this knowledge to reading words and interesting texts. Effective phonics instruction has the following key characteristics:

Early

The process of learning to read begins early in the preschool years with the development of oral language and an understanding of the functions of print. In kindergarten, children should be taught to accurately identify the letters of the alphabet. Children's alphabet knowledge is enhanced when they are engaged in activities where they learn to identify and name both upper case and lower case letters through games, songs, and activities that encourage them to practice writing the letters they are learning.

Additional Resources

In addition to alphabet knowledge, children in kindergarten need to develop their phonemic awareness, progressing from identifying rhyming words and creating rhymes to learning that sentences are made up of separate words. They then learn that words are composed of syllables and of sounds that can be separated from each other, and manipulated and used in other words.

As children acquire knowledge of the alphabet and begin to hear and play with the sounds in words, they are ready for early instruction in associating letters and sounds, phonics. The benefit of phonics instruction in kindergarten is documented in the recent report of the National Reading Panel (2000): "The ability to read and spell was enhanced in kindergartners who received systematic phonics instruction" (p. 9). The report also states: "Although conventional wisdom has suggested that kindergarten students might not be ready for phonics, this assumption was not supported by the data. The effects of systematic early phonics instruction were significant and substantial in kindergarten and first grade, indicating that systematic phonics programs should be implemented at those age and grade levels" (p. 10).

Systematic

Systematic phonics instruction refers to instruction that follows a carefully planned sequence; however, there is no one "correct" sequence for phonics instruction. Rather, there are logical principles that should guide a scope and sequence for teaching phonics. Those principles involve:

a. Moving from easier to more difficult instructional activities. For example, introducing the sound for letters like *m* and *s* early because their sounds can be elongated and emphasized (it is easy to say *mmm*) as contrasted with the sounds for *t* or *b,* which cannot be held.

b. Teaching in a sequence in which most useful information is taught early and less useful information is taught later. For example, teaching the sounds for *t* and *m* before the sounds for *j* and *y* because many more words contain *t* and *m*.

c. Introducing consonants and vowels in a sequence that permits children to read words.

d. Introducing consonant digraphs and blends/clusters after single consonants are taught.

e. Providing blending instruction with words that contain the sound-letter relationships that the children are learning.

f. Providing practice opportunities that include new sound-letter relationships as well as cumulative review of previously taught relationships. It is particularly important that children have opportunities to read texts that contain words that use recently taught phonics elements—often referred to as decodable texts.

Direct-Explicit

Phonics instruction is usually categorized as explicit or implicit. The National Reading Panel (2000) analysis indicated that "explicit, systematic phonics instruction is a valuable and essential part of a successful classroom reading program" (p. 10). In explicit phonics instruction, the sounds associated with the letters are identified in isolation and then blended together to form words. The teacher directly tells students the sound represented by an individual letter. For example, "The letter *s* makes the sound */sss/*." When children have learned several letter/sound correspondences, including one or two vowels, they can read words by blending the sounds for the letters together. For example, students who have learned the sound-letter correspondences */s/ /a/* and */t/* can blend them to read *sat.*

On the other hand, the National Reading Panel defined implicit (also called analytic phonics) as: "teaching students to analyze letter-sound relations in previously learned words to avoid pronouncing sounds in isolation" (p. 8).

The issue of whether phonics should be taught explicitly or implicitly has been among the most hotly debated topics in the field of reading. Critics of explicit phonics charge that many consonant sounds cannot be produced without distorting them by adding a vowel sound to make them pronounceable, e.g., in an attempt to blend the phonemes in *cup,* a child could add a schwa sound, which would result in something like */k/ /0/ /ù/ /p/ /0/* and go unrecognized as *cup* by the novice reader. On the other hand, the 1985 Commission on Reading (Anderson, et al. 1985) points out that implicit phonics approaches, where sounds are never isolated, where instead children are told statements like *m* has the sound heard at the beginning of mother, places very high phonemic segmentation demands on beginning readers, many of whom have difficulty with this skill. What can be concluded from research studies and reviews?

More than three decades ago Jeanne Chall (1967), based on her research review, concluded that explicit phonics is more effective and affirmed this position in her 1983 publication. The 1985 Commission on Reading (Anderson, et al. 1985), though cautious, arrived at the following conclusion: "In the judgment of the Commission, isolating sounds associated with most letters and teaching children to blend the sounds of the letters together to try to identify words are useful, constructive strategies. These are the strategies of explicit phonics" (p. 42). The Commission goes on to urge flexibility in phonics instruction. After examining all the reliable available evidence, the National Reading Panel (2000) concluded that explicit (synthetic) phonics has a positive and significant effect for low socio-economic-status children and for children who have difficulty learning to read. Thus, the major research reviews of beginning reading instruction support teaching phonics explicitly.

Flexible and Strategic

Finally, an efficient phonics program adjusts the form and intensity of instruction to the needs of children who are learning to read; different children seem to need varying amounts of phonics instruction and practice. Consequently, frequent diagnostic checks should be part of instruction. While some students will quickly master decoding skills, others will require reteaching and appropriate forms of added practice.

In an efficient decoding program, teachers will model the various decoding processes for students, and demonstrate how these processes can be applied flexibly and strategically during the reading of real texts so that students will understand how to apply the decoding skills they have and to strategically use multiple sources of information to confirm a meaning suggested by an analysis of an unfamiliar word. Starting in first

grade, teachers may begin to use think alouds to demonstrate for students how skilled readers approach new words. To be effective, these think-aloud models should demonstrate how the reader identifies familiar chunks or word parts within the word and then applies a "sounding out" strategy, reading the sounds and parts from left to right.

Extended

Decoding skills strategies should be flexible and grow as readers grow. In the middle and upper elementary grades, the strategy includes decoding

> **Proficient reading is essential for success in today's world, and efficient decoding skills are essential, though not sufficient, for proficient reading.**

multisyllabic words through dividing words into syllables and through the identification of base words and word roots, and prefixes and suffixes.

Students need instruction and guidance in decoding even as they move beyond the initial stages of learning to read. As they encounter longer words, one of their greatest challenges is to divide those words into pronounceable syllables. While mature readers, because of much practice in decoding, develop

"a sense" of where to divide words they have not seen before (Adams, 1990), developing readers may need to be taught to flexibly and strategically use a small number of useful generalizations for dividing words and pronouncing syllables. For example, a third grader encountering the word *suddenly* in print for the first time might have difficulty with the beginning part of the word but recognize *ly* as a common ending; knowing that the beginning part of the word has the pattern of a vowel followed by two consonants and another vowel (referred to as a VCCV pattern) and that words with this pattern often divide between the two consonants, can serve as a useful next step to decoding the word; now there are two short syllables to read, *sud* and *den* which are easily pronounced by analogy, recognition of word parts, or sequential decoding. Notice, however, that the vowel sound in the second syllable needs to be adjusted to get at the real word *suddenly*. This also illustrates that meaning, deciding the tentative pronunciation arrived at through decoding, and flexibly adjusting the pronunciation, is a very important aspect of decoding.

Much of students' learning of sight words and of strategies for decoding longer and often more structurally complex words is related to their vocabulary growth. Students must read widely; and if, in addition, they understand how word parts combine to create words, they have at their disposal one of the most powerful strategies for not only decoding new words in reading but also for increasing their vocabularies.

Conclusions

Proficient reading is essential for success in today's world, and efficient decoding skills are essential, though not sufficient,

Additional Resources

for proficient reading. Students who fail to develop fluent decoding will not be proficient readers nor are they likely to succeed in school. Recent research, particularly major research syntheses (Adams, 1990; Learning First Alliance, 1998; National Reading Panel, 2000; Snow, et al., 1998) provides informed guidance about instructional practices that lead to the development of efficient decoding skills. Decoding skills need to build on a foundation of oral language and phonemic and orthographic awareness in children who understand the functions and value of reading. Early phonics instruction develops an understanding of the alphabetic principle and helps young children make use of the orderly relationship that exists between letters and sounds. Effective phonics instruction leads developing readers to systematically process print through sequential decoding and, through that processing, to develop the ability to rapidly recognize common groups of letters and whole words. Wide reading extends the rapid recognition of word parts and words. This fluency allows the maturing reader to focus attention on actively constructing and responding to the meaning of print.

Well over a decade ago, Keith Stanovich (1986; also see Cunningham & Stanovich, 1998) published what has become a classic article in the field of reading. He made the all-important point that students who receive excellent decoding instruction are off to a fast start in reading and are motivated to read widely. That wide reading, in turn, further enhances the development of reading skills and achievement of those students. Conversely, students with poor decoding skills are motivated to avoid reading and their failure to read limits the development of their reading skills and achievement. As a consequence, the gap between achieving and non-achieving readers widens as they progress through school. In other words, "The rich get richer and the poor get poorer." Thus decoding fluency is of monumental importance in that it unlocks the world of reading. ■

Author

David J. Chard is Associate Professor at the University of Oregon, where he serves as Director of Graduate Studies for Special Education. His current research and teaching focuses on the instruction of early literacy for all students, including those with learning disabilities and those at risk for school failure. Dr. Chard has published extensively on instructional interventions, improvement of teacher development programs, and word recognition processes in reading development. He has taught elementary and secondary school in Michigan and California, and in the U.S. Peace Corps in southern Africa. Dr. Chard is Past-President of the Division for Research at the Council for Exceptional Children and is a member of the International Academy of Research on Learning Disabilities. He is an author of *Houghton Mifflin Reading*.

John J. Pikulski is Professor of Education at the University of Delaware, where he has been Director of the Reading Center, Department Chairperson, and President of the University Faculty Senate. He has served as a reading and psychological consultant to numerous school districts and reading and governmental agencies throughout North America. His current research interests focus on strategies for preventing reading problems and the teaching and developing of vocabulary. An active member in the International Reading Association, Dr. Pikulski has served on its Board of Directors, chaired various committees, contributed a monthly column to its journal, and was president of the association in 1997-98. He is the coauthor of *The Diagnosis, Correction, and Prevention of Reading Disabilities* and *Informal Reading Inventories*, and has been inducted into the prestigious Reading Hall of Fame. Dr. Pikulski is a senior author of *Houghton Mifflin Reading*.

Shane Templeton is Foundation Professor of Curriculum and Instruction at the University of Nevada, Reno. Dr. Templeton's research has focused on developmental word knowledge in elementary, middle, and high school students. His books include *Children's Literacy: Contexts for Meaningful Learning* and *Teaching the Integrated Language Arts*. He is coauthor of *Words Their Way: Word Study for Phonics, Vocabulary, and Spelling Instruction*.

Dr. Templeton is the senior author of *Houghton Mifflin Spelling and Vocabulary* and an author of *Houghton Mifflin English* and *Houghton Mifflin Reading*. Since 1987, Dr. Templeton has been a member of the Usage Panel of the *American Heritage Dictionary*.

> "...reading comprehension has come to be viewed as the 'essence of reading'"
>
> — *National Reading Panel, 2000, p. 4-1*

Understanding and Supporting Comprehension Development in the Elementary and Middle Grades

Marjorie Y. Lipson and J. David Cooper

Introduction

Although educators often disagree about many other aspects of literacy, there appears to be universal agreement that the primary goal and purpose of reading is to comprehend text—to understand what we read. Even more impressively, there is a consensus about the nature of comprehension. Comprehension is not just the by-product of accurate word recognition. Instead, we know that comprehension is a complex process which requires active and intentional cognitive effort on the part of the reader.

Figure 4

NARRATIVES	Story Structure
FANTASY	*Julius,* Anfela Johnson *Lost and Found,* Mark Teague
REALISTIC FICTION	*Mariah Keeps Cool,* M.P. Walter *The View from Saturday,* E.L. Konigsburg
HISTORICAL FICTION	*By the Shores of Silver Lake,* L.I. Wilder
FOLK TALES	*The Great Ball Game,* J. Bruchac
MYSTERY	*Encyclopedia Brown, The Case of the Earthenware Pig,* D. Sobol

EXPOSITION	Text Structure
CAUSE-EFFECT	*Wildfires,* S.Simon *Passage to Freedom,* K. Mochizuki
COMPARE/CONTRAST	*Chuck Close Up Close,* Chuck Close
DESCRIPTION	*Ants,* R. Stefoff *Anthony Reynoso: Born to Rope,* G. Gordon
TIME ORDER	*Nights of the Pufflings,* B. McMillan

TEXT ORGANIZATION

Adjunct Aids (illustrations, headings, boldfaced type, charts, figures, maps, summaries, etc.)

Coherence and Unity (devices to help clarify, connect, and relate the ideas in text — e.g. connectives, pronouns, linking words)

Development: Prior Knowledge, Background Experience, and Vocabulary

It is difficult to over-estimate the influence of children's prior knowledge and their experience. In their review of children's learning from text, Alexander and Jetton (2000) conclude: "Of all the factors (involved in learning from text), none exerts more influence on what students understand and remember than the knowledge they possess" (p. 291).

Over the past three decades, research findings have consistently demonstrated how prior knowledge and experience influence reading comprehension (Lipson, 1982, 1983). Simply put, the more accurate and elaborated knowledge readers have about the ideas, concepts, or events described in the text, the better they will understand it. On the other hand, limited information and/or misconceptions create obstacles to comprehension. When people (not just children or poor readers) read unfamiliar text, they read more slowly, they remember less, they construct meanings that are inconsistent with the author's, and they sometimes reject the text information outright.

In their important book, *Preventing Reading Difficulties in Young Children* (Snow & Griffin, 1998), a panel of nationally renowned experts concluded that

> The breadth and depth of a child's literacy experiences determine not only how many and what kinds of words she or he will encounter but also the background knowledge

Additional Resources

with which a child can conceptualize the meaning of any new word and the orthographic knowledge that frees that meaning from the printed page. Every opportunity should be taken to extend and enrich children's background knowledge and understanding in every way possible, for the ultimate significance and memorability of any word or text depends on whether children possess the background knowledge and conceptual sophistication to understand its meaning.
(p. 219)

This conclusion highlights the strong connection between readers' prior knowledge and their vocabulary development.

The importance of vocabulary development as a major contributor to reading comprehension has long been acknowledged and widely studied (See Beck, McKeown, & Omanson, 1999). In *Preventing Reading Difficulties in Young Children,* the authors describe why vocabulary development might predict reading comprehension:

> Written text places high demands on vocabulary knowledge. Even the words used in children's books are more rare than those used in adult conversations and prime time television. Learning new concepts and words that encode them is essential to comprehension development. (Snow, Burns, & Griffin, 1998, p. 217)

There is a reciprocal relationship between readers' prior knowledge/

vocabulary development and their ability to read and understand a wide variety of texts. Not surprisingly, the research suggests that English Language Learners (ELL) " . . . who develop a strong linguistic and cognitive base in their primary language tend to transfer those attitudes and skills to the other language and culture (they are learning)" (Ovando, 1993, p. 225) and are more successful at learning to read and write in English (Hudleson, 1987).

Good prior knowledge and appropriate experiences certainly enhance comprehension; but wide and engaging reading also expands vocabulary and promotes conceptual development. The massive amounts of vocabulary that children need to learn and that most do learn has led many researchers to the conclusion that most vocabulary must be acquired incidentally through wide, frequent reading. There is evidence that reading materials are far richer in vocabulary content than oral language. There is also some evidence that students can be taught strategies that increase their ability to derive the meaning of words that they encounter in their reading.

Experience with books helps develop students' vocabulary, but it also helps children to develop a different sort of prior knowledge, equally important for comprehension. Young children often do not fully understand how stories work—especially complex stories with multiple problems. Researchers have found that young children often understand and remember only some parts of stories (Lipson, Mosenthal, & Mekkelsen, 1999).

As children grow, they read and hear increasingly complex texts, and they become more able to grasp the subtler aspects of them. Not surprisingly, chil-

dren not only understand them better while reading, but they are also more likely to include these components in their own writing. By sixth grade, young readers and writers should be able to use a wide range of knowledge, extensive vocabulary, and broad experience to understand and write texts.

The Influence of Text: Understanding Different Types of Texts

Even when readers have much experience and good prior knowledge, their comprehension varies depending on the type of text they are reading. Certainly it is no surprise that "harder" material is more difficult to understand than "easier" material. But what makes a text harder or easier to read and understand?

Some of the factors are important for all readers, and others are more important for beginning readers than for more mature and highly skilled readers. For example, the relationship between the pictures and text can make a big difference in how well very young children understand a story. Indeed, research suggests that pictured events and concepts are significantly more likely to be recalled than non-pictured events (Lipson et al., 1999). If the pictures are central to and support the main themes and ideas of the story, this is good. If, however, the pictures are not supportive, or draw children's attention to unimportant side events (called "seductive details") this can pose problems (Alexander & Jetton, 2000). Older, more mature readers do not rely so heavily on pictures to comprehend the stories/texts they read.

Some features of text influence comprehension for all readers. Aspects of text such as its structure, complexity, and genre affect understanding even when readers are very accurate decoders (Goldman & Rakestraw, 2000; Lipson et al., 1999).

Text Structures: Narrative

Generally speaking, we organize texts in two large categories: narrative (stories) and exposition (explanation of facts and concepts). These two types of text are different in both purpose and organization (see Figure 4, page 65). For example, people generally read stories for entertainment, although we may learn from them as well. We read expository text to learn new or clarify old information, although these texts can be extremely interesting and entertaining.

Narratives typically share a common set of features and structures called a "story grammar" (Stein & Glenn, 1979). Readers who understand how stories are organized can use this information to help them understand better. When the features of narrative texts are "mapped," children often read and comprehend the stories better and more easily. All narrative texts have

- A setting, either physical or psychological (time/place/mental state)
- Characters, the major players in the story
- A problem, or initiating event, something that gets the story started
- Important events, related to the problem
- An outcome or resolution, events or consequences that resolve the problem.

In addition, most narratives have a theme, a major idea or important concept that the author is trying to convey. There may be more than one theme in a complex narrative, and these ideas are generally more universal than concrete

(e.g. "friends stand by each other and help out when needed").

Although children often find narratives easier to read, they may not always understand the more subtle aspects of stories such as the motives or goals of characters or the theme of the story. In addition, there are different genres of narrative texts, and children do not usually have extensive experience with all these different types of stories. For example, they may be quite comfortable reading and understanding simple realistic fiction, but they may not have encountered historical fiction or more sophisticated fantasies. Both exposure and good instruction are usually needed

Additional Resources

to help children read and understand a broad range of different genres.

Text Structures: Exposition

Expository texts are organized differently than narratives because they are written for a different purpose (see Figure 4). We read exposition to learn new information, about a different point of view, or to clarify confusions.

The ideas within a text can be organized in a number of different ways. Teachers and children often focus on the sequence of events and, indeed, these are important in many narrative stories. In exposition, however, the major ideas and events in the text are often not organized according to sequence, but rather by some other text structure.

Not all text structures are equally easy to understand. Stories tend to be easier to understand than exposition for many young readers and, within expository texts, certain organizational patterns are easier than others (Armbruster, 1984). For example, cause-effect is more challenging for children than sequence (see graphic organizers in the discussion of Instruction below).

How Do Children Comprehend?

Not too long ago, both reading experts and teachers assumed that reading comprehension occurred as a natural by-product of accurate word recognition. However, over the past three decades researchers have pointed to a more complicated explanation. There is strong agreement that comprehension is a complex cognitive activity that relies on excellent fluency, vocabulary, and prior knowledge. In addition, "active interactive strategic processes are critically necessary to the development of reading comprehension. . . . " (National Reading Panel, p. 4-11). Good

readers intend to understand—it is not a passive activity that occurs without effort. Teachers and students alike must understand the active, purposeful nature of comprehension.

The Role of Strategies

Reading ability—both comprehension and word recognition—is facilitated when readers use strategies. Even very young children can and do employ strategies during reading, so a solid reading program should introduce and sustain a strategic approach to reading throughout grades K–6. For children in grades 4–8, strategic reading is absolutely essential. The texts and tasks that readers regularly encounter in those grades are more conceptually demanding, are more complex in both form and function, and often address topics or domain knowledge that is unfamiliar. Importantly, even able readers can benefit from explicit instruction and effective instructional support (National Reading Panel, 2000, p. 4–47).

The obvious next question is, "Are there some strategies that really help readers and writers to be more competent—to read and write better?" The answer is clearly "Yes," although the particular list of essential strategies might vary slightly from one educator or researcher to another. There are two things that most experts agree are essential to understand. First, the number of these strategies is small—it isn't a long list of discrete abilities. Second, these strategies, individually, are not as important as a "strategic approach." As Dole and others have argued, "The goal of instruction would be to develop (in students) a sense of conscious control, or metacognitive awareness, over a set of strategies that they can adapt to any

text they read" (emphasis added Dole et al., p, 242).

Becoming strategic is a developmental process; it occurs over time as students encounter increasingly difficult texts and new situations. The same relatively small set of strategies emerges quite early in children's development. Among the most highly useful strategies are (1) making predictions and drawing inferences; (2) self-questioning; (3) monitoring comprehension; (4) summarizing; and (5) evaluating. These strategies, individually, are not as important as a "strategic approach" which allows readers to respond differently to different topics, text, genres, and tasks.

Effective comprehenders often use several strategies at one time. In addition, good readers use strategies in a flexible manner. Reading requires the orchestration of a number of skills and strategies.

The Skill and Strategy Connection

According to Pearson, Dole, and their colleagues (1991/1992), strategies are "conscious and flexible plans that readers apply and adapt to a variety of texts and tasks. . . . Skills, by contrast, are viewed as highly routinized, almost automatic behaviors" (Dole, Duffy, Roehler, & Pearson, 1991, p. 242). Skills are generally thought to be less complex than strategies which, in fact, generally require the orchestration of several skills.

For example, while summarizing is an effective comprehension strategy, readers cannot summarize texts well without an array of skills. Summarization is likely to help young readers understand and appreciate Mark Teague's lovely fantasy, *Lost and Found*. However, in order to do this successfully, children would need to pay careful attention to the sequence of events and they need to note surprising details.

Strategies require using several skills or abilities in concert. Individual skills can be very important under some circumstances, but they are generally not, by themselves, sufficient to accomplish the complex jobs required of mature readers and writers. No one set of skills is always linked to a particular strategy. Instead, strategies comprise skill combinations which involve a degree of critical thinking, thoughtful selection, and self-control that is not true for skills. Thus, they are cognitively more complex, but also more versatile.

As important as strategies are, they generally are not acquired without at least some explicit instruction and attention from the teacher. Effective and mature readers can recruit a variety of skills under any number of circumstances to respond to the varying demands of different texts and different tasks. Even highly skilled readers may not have a flexible and strategic approach to reading. Unlike other aspects of reading, exposure and experience alone do not appear to ensure controlled knowledge and use of strategies.

What Should Comprehension Instruction Look Like?

Fortunately, students can acquire fluency, learn to be strategic, and learn to comprehend more deeply. Even better, we have fairly good information about the type of instruction that promotes good comprehension in students. It is very clear that extensive reading practice is essential in building both fluency and knowledge. It is equally clear that good, explicit instruction in some areas provides additional benefit to students. The National Reading Panel (2000) concluded that there are eight

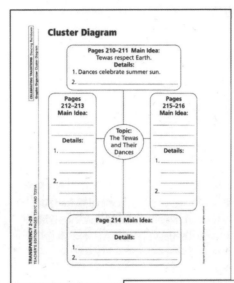

Figure 5

types of instruction that are especially effective in teaching students to comprehend. We will discuss each of these types of instruction (highlighted below) within this somewhat broader framework of instruction:

- Reading Opportunity
- Instructional Support for Comprehension in which we discuss **(1) graphic organizers** and **(2) story structure,** but also pre-reading activities and guided reading and questioning strategies; and fluency
- Explicit Instruction in which we discuss **(3) comprehension monitoring, (4) summarizing,** and **(5) multiple-strategy teaching**
- The Added Value of Discussion, in which we describe appropriate **(6) cooperative learning** opportunities for reading

instruction and also discuss **(7) question answering** and **(8) question generation approaches**

Provide Extensive Opportunities for Exposure and Practice

Both our own common sense and decades of research highlight the importance of practice in learning to read. There is a strong association between voluntary reading and writing and general reading and writing achievement (Greaney, 1980; Morrow, 1983). The amount of time children spend reading books is strongly linked to reading comprehension and reading achievement gains (Anderson, Wilson, & Fielding, 1988; Taylor, Frye, & Maruyama, 1990).

What may not be quite so evident is how important reading practice is to developing both the ability to comprehend and general cognitive competence. As Stanovich (1992) has argued, ". . . reading does make people smarter" (pg. 226). In part, this conclusion comes from the fact that wide reading promotes vocabulary development. Research summaries by two recent commissions concluded that both overall exposure to print and independent reading promote and develop vocabulary, reading fluency, and comprehension (National Reading Panel, 2000; Snow, Burns, & Griffin, 1998). Importantly, " . . . exposure to print is efficacious regardless of the level of the child's cognitive and reading abilities. We do not have to wait for 'pre-requisite' abilities to be in place before encouraging free reading" (Stanovich, 1992, p. 226).

Recent research also suggests that extensive reading practice as part of a planned instructional program is a distinguished characteristic of successful

schools in all demographic regions. In successful schools, primary grade children engaged in continuous text reading between 20 and 30 minutes each day, while intermediate grade children read as much as an hour a day (see Lipson et al., 2000; Taylor & Pearson, in press). In less successful schools, the amount of text reading time was significantly less. Therefore, effective reading programs must include ample opportunity for students to read appropriately-leveled texts. To accomplish this, classrooms must include a large and accessible collection of books (Morrow et. al., 1999; Mosenthal et al, in press; Neuman, 1999).

Students must read and create authentic materials if they are going to become genuinely strategic (Brown, Collins, & Deguid, 1989; Duffy, 1993; Resnick, 1987). Although short, contrived texts can be helpful in introducing a skill or strategy to students, students will not be able to develop effective comprehension strategies like monitoring, summarizing, and self-questioning unless they are reading increasingly complex mate-

rial of appropriately substantial length. Nor will they develop and acquire the rich vocabulary and broad understanding of text structure required to become a reader with excellent comprehension.

This balance is especially delicate in the early grades and for students acquiring English as a second language (ESL), when they may not be able to read materials that will challenge and develop their comprehension abilities and background knowledge. Consequently, many authors recommend using teacher read alouds for comprehension instruction while at the same time using more controlled text for beginning readers to practice word-level skills and strategies (Honig, Diamond, & Gutlohn, 2000).

Importantly, different materials require different approaches, combinations, and degrees of effort. The flexible and intentional aspects of strategy instruction really only develop when students read (or hear) fine literature, excellent nonfiction, and a wide range of other real-world materials.

Support Comprehension. Because opportunity and experience are so central to the development of vocabulary and comprehension, teachers must find ways to provide access to texts. Independent reading of texts is important, and a regular silent or quiet reading time should be a part of every classroom routine. In addition, however, teachers need to support students so that they can read and comprehend materials that are just out of their independent reach.

Teachers can support students' comprehension by providing support for reading before they begin reading; by building background, introducing key vocabulary, and activating existing knowledge. Good instruction should involve solid pre-reading engagement with ideas, words, and organizational schemes so that students' comprehension is improved. According to Anderson et al. (1985), "Using instructional time to build background knowledge pays dividends in comprehension" and "useful approaches to building background knowledge prior to a reading lesson focus on the concepts that will be central to understanding the upcoming story, concepts that children either do not possess or may not think of without prompting" (p. 50). Although none of these instructional activities is new or novel, teachers usually do not spend enough time on these parts of their instructional plan.

In addition, teachers can enhance students' understanding through instructional scaffolding. Scaffolding had been described as any assistance that allows someone to solve a problem, carry out a task, or achieve a goal that he or she could not accomplish without support (Wood, Bruner, and Ross, 1976). Graphic organizers and visual maps are among the very best types of scaffolding for literacy (National Reading Panel, 2000).

For narrative texts, story maps work very well. At first, children can be taught a generic map that includes the major elements of story grammar (see earlier discussion of stories). Later on, children can be supported in reading more complex stories by providing maps that frame the particular story they are reading. Sometimes stories are best understood by attending to relationships among the events and not in terms of classic story grammar.

Expository texts are often more complex and variable, so graphic organizers can be especially helpful to young or less-skilled readers. Again, it is important to make sure that the graphic organizer highlights the major organizational pattern of the specific text being read so that the children's comprehension is supported as they "fill in" the parts that will guide them through the selection (see Figure 5, page 69). The cluster diagram in Figure 5 reveals the main idea and supporting detail structure of the text *Dancing Rainbows,* about Native American traditional dances. Although this structure is common among nonfiction texts, the organizer is not generic; rather, it matches the selection exactly and will, therefore, be more helpful especially for students who are struggling readers. As children gain expertise, they should be encouraged to create their graphic depictions of the material they are reading.

Not all children need extensive support during reading, and the degree of support will likely vary depending on the type of text and the students' familiarity with the content of the piece. Many ELL students can benefit from enhanced support. For students who need it, teachers can help promote comprehension by supplying additional information about vocabulary and key concepts; can model appropriate comprehension strategy use or support students' efforts to use strategies themselves; and can prompt discussion through skillful use of questioning (see discussion below).

A comprehensive reading program should include provisions for flexible and varied supported guided reading of text and effective graphic supports. In addition, it should highlight key concepts and build background for students who need it. The program should also make provisions for text rereadings sing tapes and/or simplified summaries for additional experience and practice.

Teach Comprehension Explicitly

Although extensive practice and good supportive reading opportunities are necessary and generally effective, they are not sufficient for many children. Many children require explicit instruction in how to comprehend.

Some students do acquire strategies and learn to use them efficiently without explicit instruction. As we noted earlier, however, sophisticated use of strategies and coordinated skills usually require explicit teaching (Paris, Lipson, & Wixson, 1983; Paris, Wasik, & Turner, 1991). A good reading program must attend to students' strategic reading development throughout the grades. Since it appears that a relatively small set of strategies is used across many ages/grades/tasks, it makes sense to teach these strategies in all grades. The strategies don't change, but students (kindergarten and first grade) can use a summary strategy, for example, that includes telling the beginning, middle, and end. By sixth grade, student summarizations would attend to character, plot, problem-solutions, and resolutions.

During explicit instruction, teachers employ a variety of techniques: direct explanation, modeling, guided practice, feedback, and application (Dickson, Collins, Simmons, and Kameenui, 1998). Direct explanation is important, because researchers have demonstrated that many students do not seem able to extract critical information from their experiences. They need the teacher to explain exactly what (strategy, e.g.) they are learning, how to use it, and why it is important. In addition, students benefit from teacher modeling of complex strategies. As teachers "think aloud" about

Additional Resources

their cognitive actions, students can see how they could replicate these activities. Guided practice is especially important, because strategic reading seems to require that students have "conditional" knowledge regarding the strategies they are learning (Paris, Lispson, & Wixson, 1983). This explicit instruction should make clear to students the value of using a particular strategy(ies) and should model for students appropriate mental processes. Then, during guided practice, teachers should let students know when and why (conditional knowledge) to use these strategies during reading and writing tasks. As children use their newly acquired strategies in supported contexts, teachers can provide feedback. Finally, children must have ample opportunities to apply the strategies to new texts so that they can acquire independence and self-control.

Discussion Provides Added Value

Researchers have recently found that literature discussion promotes motivation for reading and can also improve students' comprehension. There are any number of possible ways to promote literature discussion, and different approaches appear to benefit children in slightly different ways. As the National Reading Panel (2000) has noted, research supports the effectiveness of cooperative grouping and also any approaches that improve students' question-answering and question-generating abilities. Two approaches to literature discussion that have strong research foundations are "Book Club", developed by Raphael and her colleagues (see McMahon, Raphael, Goatley, & Pardo, 1997) and "Question the Author" (QtA) developed by Isabel Back and her colleagues (Beck et al.,

1996; Beck, McKeown, Hamiliton, & Kucan, 1997).

Whereas discussion is just one component of Book Club, it is the major feature of QtA. Since the primary purpose for QtA is to help students build understanding from text to increase and improve comprehension, we will describe this approach in some detail. The research base for QtA is impressive. Beck et al, (1996) report that, in QtA classrooms, teacher questions and student responses become more meaning-oriented and that students become more active participants in discussion. In addition, when students responded to teacher queries, they were more likely than other readers to go beyond verbatim responses, integrating their own prior knowledge, inferences, or hypotheses in their answers. Importantly, during discussions, students were also much more likely to initiate their own questions and comments.

Conclusion

Successful comprehension instruction requires a sophisticated literacy program, one that includes: diverse literature, both fiction and nonfiction; many opportunities for independent and supported practice; thoughtful instruction before, during, and after reading; explicit teaching of comprehension skills and strategies; and cooperative, collaborative discussion of texts. Because there is such overwhelming consensus about good, research-based instruction in the area of comprehension, educators should expect their commercial programs to support effective practice in each of these areas. ■

Authors

Dr. Marjorie Lipson is Professor of Education at the University of Vermont where she has been on the faculty since 1985. Her areas of specialty in research and scholarship include reading comprehension, issues in reading assessment, and assessment/instruction of students with reading disabilities. She has served on several editorial advisory boards of academic journals, and she is author of the book *Assessment and Instruction of Reading and Writing Disabilities: An Interactive Approach.* Dr. Lipson is also an author of *Houghton Mifflin Reading: A Legacy of Literacy.*

Dr. J. David Cooper is Adjunct Professor of Education at Ball State University, where he has been Professor and Director of Reading. Dr. Cooper is the author of *Literacy: Helping Children Construct Meaning* (5th edition) and *Improving Reading Comprehension*, and co-author of *The What and How of Reading Instruction* and several other professional books. He is author of a new book, *Literacy Assessment: Helping Teachers Plan Instruction.* For the last six years, Dr. Cooper has been conducting research and developing programs on reading intervention for students in grades 3–8. He has been a reviewer for several professional journals, and he is a member of numerous professional organizations, including the International Reading Association. Dr. Cooper is Senior Author for *Soar to Success* and *Houghton Mifflin Reading: A Legacy of Literacy.*

Bibliography

Understanding Assessment: Putting Together the Puzzle

Andrade, H.G. (2000). Using rubrics to promote thinking and learning. *Educational Leadership,* 57, 13-18.

Blair, J. & Archer, J. (2001). NEA members denounce high-stakes testing. http://www.edweek.org/ew/ews-tory.cfm?slug=42neatest_web. h20&keywords=National%20Education%20Association

Brennan, R.T., Kim, J., Wenz-Gross, M., & Siperstein, G.N. (2001). The relative equitability of high-stakes testing versus teacher-assigned grades: An analysis of the Massachusetts Comprehensive Assessment System (MCAS). *Harvard Educational Review,* 71, 173-216.

Education Week (2001). A Better Balance: Standards, Tests, and the Tools to Succeed. 20(17), Jan 11, 2001.

Graue, M. E. (1993). Integrating theory and practice through instructional assessment. *Educational Assessment,* 1(4), 283-310.

Hiebert, E. H., & Calfee, R. C. (1989). Advancing academic literacy through teachers' assessments. *Educational Leadership,* 46(7), 50-54.

Hiebert, E. H., Valencia, S. W., & Afflerbach, P. P. (1994). Understand authentic reading assessment: Definitions and perspectives. In S. W. Valencia, E. H. Hiebert, & P. P. Afflerbach (Eds.), *Authentic reading assessment: Practices and possibilities,* (pp. 6-21). Newark, DE: International Reading Association. International Reading Association. (1999).

International Reading Association. (1982). *Misuse of grade equivalents. The Reading Teacher,* 35(4) 464.

Jenkins, J.R., Johnson, E., & Hileman, J. (2000). Sources of individual differences on the new reading performance assessments. Unpublished manuscript.

Johnston, P.H. & Winograd, P.N. (1985). Passive failure in reading. Journal of Reading Behavior, 17(4), 279-301.

Linn, R. L. (2000). Assessments and accountability. *Educational Researcher,* 29(2), 4-16.

National Research Council (1999). Testing, teaching, and learning: A guide for states and school districts. Committee on Title I Testing and Assessment, R.F. Elmore & R. Rothstein (Eds.). Board on Testing and Assessment, Commission on Behavioral and Social Sciences and Education. Washington, DC: National Academy Press.

Orlofsky, G.F. & Olson, L. (2001). The state of the states. Education Week, 20(17), 86-108, Jan 11, 2001.

Pearson, P. D., & Valencia, S. W. (1987). Assessment, accountability, and professional prerogative. In J. E. Readence & R. S. Baldwin (Eds.), Research in literacy: Merging perspectives, (pp. 3-16). Rochester, NY: National Reading Conference.

Popham, J.W. (1999). Why standardized test scores don't measure educational quality. Educational Leadership, 56(6), 8-15.

Rief, L. (1990). Finding the value in evaluation: Self-evaluation in a middle school classroom. Educational Leadership, 47(6), 24-29.

Shavelson, R. J. & Stern, P. (1981). Research on teachers pedagogical thoughts, judgments, decisions and behavior. Review of Educational Research, 51(4), 455-498.

Shepard, L.A. (1999). The role of assessment in a learning culture. Educational Researcher, 29(7), 4-14.

Stiggins, R. J. (1997). Student-centered classroom assessment. 2nd edition. Upper Saddle River, N.J.: Merrill.

Stiggins, R.J. & Conklin, N.F. (1992). In teachers' hands. Investigating the practices of classroom assessment. Albany, NY: State University of New York Press.

Valencia, S.W. (1998). Literacy portfolios in action. Belmont, CA: Wadsworth.

Valencia, S. W. & Place, N. (1994). Literacy portfolios for teaching, learning, and accountability: The Bellevue literacy assessment project. In S. W. Valencia, E. H. Hiebert, & P. P. Afflerbach (Eds.), Authentic reading assessment; Practices and possibilities, . Newark, DE: International Reading Association.

Wiggins, G. (1998). Educative assessment : Designing assessments to inform and improve student performance. San Francisco, CA: Jossey-Bass.

Wiggins, G. (1989). A true test: Toward more authentic and equitable assessment. Phi Delta Kappan, 79(7), 703-713.

Teaching and Developing Vocabulary: Key to Long-Term Reading Success

Anderson, R.C. (1996). Research foundations to support wide reading. In Creany, V. (Ed.), Promoting reading in developing countries, 55–77. Newark, DE: International Reading Association.

Anderson, R.C., and Freebody, P. (1981). Vocabulary knowledge. In J. Guthrie (Ed.), Comprehension and teaching: Research reviews, 77–117. Newark, DE: International Reading Association.

Anderson, R.C., Hiebert, E. H., Scott, J.A., and Wilkerson, I.A. (1985). Becoming a nation of readers. Washington, D.C.: National Institute of Education.

Aronoff, M. (1994). Morphology. In A. C. Purves, L. Papa, and S. Jordan (Eds.), Encyclopedia of English studies and language arts, Vol. 2, 820–821. New York: Scholastic.

Bear, D.R., Ivernizzi, M., Templeton, S., and Johnston, F. (2004) Words their way: Word study for phonics, vocabulary, and spelling instruction. Upper Saddle River, NJ: Merrill/Prentice Hall.

Beck, I. L., McKeown, M. G., and Kucan, L. (2002). Bringing words to life: Robust vocabulary instruction. New York: Guilford.

Cunningham, A.E. and Stanovich, K.E. (1998). What reading does for the mind. American Educator, Summer, 8–15.

Durkin, D. (1979). What classroom instruction has to say about reading comprehension instruction. Reading Research Quarterly, 14, 481–533.

Ehri, L.C. (1994). Development of the ability to read words: Update. In R. Ruddell, M. Ruddell, and H. Singer (Eds.), Theoretical models and processes of reading (4th ed.), 323–358. Hillsdale, NJ: Erlbaum.

Ehri, L.C. (1998). Grapheme-phoneme knowledge is essential for learning to read words in English. In J.L. Metsala and L.C. Ehri (Eds.), Word recognition in beginning literacy, 3–40. Mahwah, NJ: Erlbaum.

Elley, W. B. (1989). Vocabulary acquisition from listening to stories. Reading Research Quarterly, 24, 174–187.

Juel, C. Biancarosa, G., Coker, D., and Deffes, R. (2003). Walking with Rosie: A cautionary tale of early reading instruction. Educational Leadership, April, 13–18.

Kuhn, M.R., and Stahl, S.A. (1998). Teaching children to learn word meanings from context: A synthesis and some questions. Journal of Literacy Research, 30, 119–138.

Nagy, W.E., and Anderson, R.C. (1984). How many words are there in printed school English? Reading Research Quarterly, 19, 304–330.

National Reading Panel. (2000). Report of the National Reading Panel: Teaching children to read. Washington, D.C.: National Institute of Child Health and Human Development.

Pikulski, J.J., and Chard, D.J. (2003). Fluency: Bridge from decoding to reading comprehension. Boston, MA: Houghton Mifflin Company.

Progress in International Reading/Literacy Study. (2003). www.pirls.org.

Rand Reading Study Group. (2002). Reading for understanding: Towards an R&D program in reading comprehension. www.rand.org/multi/achievementforall

Templeton, S. (1989). Tacit and explicit knowledge of derivational morphology: Foundations for a unified approach to spelling and vocabulary development in the intermediate grades and beyond. Reading Psychology, 10, 233–253.

Templeton, S. (2003a). Spelling. In J. Flood, D. Lapp, J. Squire, and J. M. Jensen (Eds.), Handbook of research on teaching the English language arts (2nd ed.), 738–751. Mahwah, NY: Lawrence Erlbaum Associates.

Templeton, S. (2003b). Teaching of spelling. In J. Guthrie (Senior Ed.), Encyclopedia of education (2nd ed.), 2302–2305. New York: Macmillan.

Additional Resources

Templeton, S. (2004). The vocabulary-spelling connection: Orthographic development and morphological knowledge at the intermediate grades and beyond. In J. Baumann and E. Kameenui (Eds.), Vocabulary instruction, 118–138. New York: Guilford Press.

Fluency: The Bridge from Decoding to Reading Comprehension

Adams, M.J. (1990). Beginning to read: Thinking and learning about print. Cambridge, MA: MIT Press.

Anderson R.C., E.H. Heibert, J.A. Scott, and I.A. Wilkerson (1985). Becoming a nation of readers: The report of the commission on reading. Washington, D.C.: The National Institute on Education.

Carver, R. P. and J.V. Hoffman (1981). "The effect of practice through repeated reading on gain in reading ability using a computer-based instructional system." Reading Research Quarterly, 16 (3), 374–390.

Chard, D.J., S. Vaughn, and B.J. Tyler (2002). "A synthesis of research on effective interventions for building fluency with elementary students with learning disabilities." Journal of Learning Disabilities, 35, 386–406.

Cohen, A.L. (1988). "An evaluation of the effectiveness of two methods for providing computer-assisted repeated reading training to reading disabled students." Doctoral dissertation, Florida State University, Tallahassee.

Cromer, W. (1970). "The difference model: A new explanation for some reading difficulties." Journal of Educational Psychology, 61, 471–483.

Cunningham, A.E. and K.E. Stanovich (1998). "What reading does for the mind." American Educator, Spring/Summer, 8–15.

Daley, E.J. and B.K. Martens (1994). "A comparison of three interventions for increasing oral reading performance: Application of the instructional hierarchy." Journal of Applied Behavior Analysis, 27, 459–469.

Dowhower, S.L. (1987). "Effects of repeated reading on second-grade transitional readers' fluency and comprehension." Reading Research Quarterly, 22, 389–406.

Dowhower, S.L. (1991). "Speaking of prosody: Fluency's unattended bedfellow." Theory Into Practice, 30 (3), 165–175.

Ehri, L.C. (1998). "Grapheme-phoneme knowledge is essential for learning to read words in English." In Word recognition in beginning literacy, J.L. Metsala and L.C. Ehri (Eds.). Mahwah, NJ: Lawrence Erlbaum.

Ehri, L.C. (1995). "Stages of development in learning to read words by sight." Journal of Research in Reading, 18, 116–125.

Fleisher, L.S., J.R. Jenkins, and D. Pany (1979–1980). "Effects on poor readers' comprehension of training in rapid decoding." Reading Research Quarterly, 15, 30–48.

Harris, T.L. and R.E. Hodges (1995). The literacy dictionary: A vocabulary of reading and writing. Newark, DE: International Reading Association.

Hiebert, E.H. and C.W. Fisher (2002). "Text matters in developing fluent reading." Submitted for publication.

Homan, S., P. Klesius, and S. Hite (1993). "Effects of repeated readings and nonrepetitive strategies on students' fluency and comprehension." Journal of Educational Research, 87, 94–99.

Houghton Mifflin (2001). Leveled Reading Passages. Boston: Houghton Mifflin Co.

Kuhn, M.R. and S.A. Stahl (2000). Fluency: A review of developmental and remedial practices. Ann Arbor, MI: Center for the Improvement of Early Reading Achievement.

Levy, B.A., B. Abello, and L. Lysynchuk (1997). "Transfer from word training to reading in context: Gains in fluency and comprehension." Learning Disability Quarterly, 20, 173–188.

Monda, L.E. (1989). "The effects of oral, silent, and listening repetitive reading on the fluency and comprehension of learning disabled students." Doctoral dissertation, Florida State University, Tallahassee.

Nathan, R.G. and K.E. Stanovich (1991). "The causes and consequences of differences in reading fluency." Theory Into Practice, 30 (3), 176–184.

National Reading Panel (2000). Teaching children to read: An evidence-based assessment of the scientific-research literature on reading and its implications for reading instruction. Washington, D.C.: National Institute of Child Health and Human Development.

O'Shea, L.J., P.T. Sindelar, and D.J. O'Shea (1987). "The effects of repeated readings and attentional cues on the reading fluency and comprehension of learning disabled readers." Learning Disabilities Research, 2, 103–109.

Pikulski, J.J. (1974). "Informal reading inventories: A critical review." The Reading Teacher, 28 (2), 253–258.

Pinnell, G.S., J.J. Pikulski, K.K. Wixson, J.R. Campbell, P.B. Gough, and A.S. Beatty (1995). Listening to children read aloud. Washington, D.C.: Office of Educational Research and Improvement, U.S. Department of Education.

Rashotte, C.A. and J.K. Torgeson (1985). "Repeated reading and reading fluency in learning disabled children." Reading Research Quarterly, 20, 180–188.

Samuels, S.J. (2002). "Reading fluency: Its development and assessment." In What research has to say about reading instruction, 3rd. ed., A.E. Farstrup and S.J. Samuels (Eds.). Newark, DE: International Reading Association.

From Phonemic Awareness to Fluency: Effective Decoding Instruction in a Research-Based Reading Program

Adams, M. J. (1990). Beginning to Read: Thinking and Learning About Print. Cambridge, MA: MIT Press.

Anderson, R. C., Hiebert, E. H., Scott, J. A., & Wilkinson, I. A. G. (1985). Becoming a Nation of Readers. The National Academy of Education & the Center for the Study of Reading.

Ehri, L. (1991). Development of the ability to read words. In R. Barr, M. Kamil, P. Mosenthal, & P. Pearson, eds. Handbook of Reading Research. (Vol II, pp. 383–417). New York: Longman.

Ehri, L. (1997). Learning to read and learning to spell are one and the same, almost. In C. Perfetti, L. Rieben, & M. Fayol, eds. Learning to spell: Research, theory, and practice across languages (pp. 237–269). Mahwah, NJ: Lawrence Erlbaum.

Ehri, L, & Wilce, L. (1985). Movement into reading: Is the first stage of printed word learning visual or phonetic? Reading Research Quarterly, 20, 163–179.

Ehri, L., & Wilce, L. (1986). The influence of spellings on speech: Are alveolar flaps /d/ or /t/? In D. Yaden & S. Templeton, eds. Metalinguistic awareness and beginning literacy (pp. 101–114) Portsmouth, NH.

Frances, D. J., Shaywitz, S. E., Stuebing, K. K., Shaywitz, B. A., & Fletcher, J. M. (1996). Developmental lag versus deficit models for reading disability: An individual growth curves analyses. Journal of Education Psychology, 88, 3–17.

Harris, T. L., & Hodges, R. E. (1995). The literacy dictionary: The vocabulary of reading and writing. Newark, DE, The International Reading Association.

Learning First Alliance (1998). Every Child Reading: An Action Plan. Learning First Alliance.

National Reading Council (1998). Preventing Reading Difficulties in Young Children. National Academy Press.National Reading Panel (2000). Report of the National Reading Panel, Teaching Children to Read. National Institutes of Health Pub. No. 00-4754.

Stanovich, K. E. (1980). Toward an interactive-compensatory model of individual differences in the development of reading fluency. Reading Research Quarterly, 16, 32–71.

Stanovich, K. E. (1986). Matthew effects in reading: Some consequences of individual differences in the acquisition of literacy. Reading Research Quarterly, 21, 360–406.

Templeton, S. (1992). Theory, nature, and pedagogy of higher order orthographic development in older students. In S. Templeton and D. R. Bear, eds. Development of orthographic knowledge and the foundation of literacy: A Memorial Festschrift for Edmund Henderson (pp. 253–277). Hillsdale, NJ: Lawrence Erlbaum Associates.

Templeton, S., & Morris, D. (2000). Spelling. In M. Kamil, P. Mosenthal, P.D. Pearson. & R. Barr, eds. Handbook of reading research: Volume 3 (pp. 525–543). Mawah, NJ: Lawrence Ellbaum Associates.

Understanding and Supporting Comprehension Development in the Elementary and Middle Grades

Alexander, P.A., & Jetton, T. L. (2000). Learning from text: A multidimensional and developmental perspective. In Kamil, M. L., Mosenthal, P. B., Pearson, P. D., & Barr, R. (Eds.), Handbook of reading research, Vol. 3 (pp. 285-310). Mahwah, NJ: Lawrence Erlbaum.

Armbruster, B. B. (1984). The problem of "inconsiderate text." In G. G. Duffy, L. R. Roehler, & J. Mason (Eds.), Comprehension instruction (pp. 202-217). NY: Longman.

Beck, I., McKeown, M. G. & Omanson, R. (1999). The effects and uses of diverse vocabulary instructional techniques. In California Reading Initiative. Read all about it? Readings to inform the profession (pg. 311-324). Sacramento, CA.: California State Board of Education.

Beck, I. L., McKeown, M. G., Worthy, J., Sandora, C. A., & Kucan, L. (1996). Question the author: A yearlong classroom implementation to engage students with text. Elementary School Journal, 96, 385-414.

Beck, I. L., McKeown, M. G., Hamilton, R. L., & Kucan, L. (1997). Question the author: An approach for enhancing student engagement with text. Newark, DE: International Reading Association.

Brown, J. S., Collins, A., & Duguid, P. (1989). Situated cognition and the culture of learning. Educational Researcher, 18, 32-42.

Dickinson, S. V., Simmons, D. C., & Kameenui, E. J. (1998). Metacognitive strategies: Research bases. In D. C. Simmons & E. J. Kammenui (Eds.), What reading research tells us about children with diverse learning needs: Bases and basics. Mahwah, NJ: Erlbaum.

Dole, J. A., Duffy, G. G., Roehley, L. R., & Pearson, P. D. (1991). Moving from the old to the new: Research on reading comprehension instruction. Review of Educational Research, 61 (2), 239-264.

Goldman, S. R., & Rakestraw, J. A. (2000). Structural aspects of constructing meaning from text. In Kamil, M.L., Mosenthal, P. B., Pearson, P.D., & Barr, R. (Eds.), Handbook of reading research, Vol. 3 (pp. 311-335). Mahwah, NJ: Lawrence Erlbaum.

Greaney, V. (1980). Factors related to amount and type of leisure reading. Reading Research Quarterly, 15, 337-357.

Honig, W., Diamond, L., & Gutlohn, L. (2000). Teaching reading sourcebook. Novato, CA: Arena Press.

Hudleson, S. (1987). The role of native language literacy in the education of language minority children. Language Arts, 64, 827-834.

Lipson, M. Y. (1982). Learning new information from text: The role of prior knowledge and reading ability. Journal of Reading Behavior, 14, 243-261.

Lipson, M. Y. & Wickizer, E. A. (1989). Promoting self-control and active reading through dialogues. Teaching Exceptional Children, 21 (2), 28-32.

Lipson, M. Y., Mosenthal, J. H., & Mekkelsen, J. (1999). The nature of comprehension among grade 2 children: Variability in retellings as a function of development, text, and task. In T. Shanahan & F. V. Rodriguez-Brown (Eds.), Forty-eighth yearbook of the National Reading Conference (pp. 104-119). Chicago, IL: National Reading Conference.

McMahon, S. I., Raphael, T. E., Goatley, V. J., & Pardo, L. S. (Eds.)(1997). The book club connection. NY: Teachers College Press.

Morrow, L. (1983). Home and school correlates of early interest in literature. Journal of Educational Research, 76, 221-230.

Morrow, L., Tracey, D. H., Woo, D. G., & Pressley, M. (1999). Characteristics of exemplary first-grade literacy instruction. The Reading Teacher, 52, 462-476.

Mosenthal, J. H., Lipson, M. Y., Sortino, S., Russ, B., & Mekkelsen, J. (in press). Lessons from successful country schools. In B. Taylor & P. D. Pearson (Eds.), Successful schools and accomplished teachers. Mahwah, NJ: Lawrence Erlbaum.

National Reading Panel (2000). Report of the National Reading Panel: Teaching children to read: An evidence-based assessment of the scientific research literature on reading and its implications for reading instruction. Washington, D. C.: National Institute of Child Health and Human Development, National Institutes of Health.

Ovando, C. J. (1993). Language diversity and education. In J. A. Banks & C. A. McGee Banks (Eds.), Multicultural education: Issues and perspectives (pp. 215-235). Boston: Allyn & Bacon.

Paris, S. G., Lipson, M. Y., & Wixson, K. K. (1983). Becoming a strategic reader. Contemporary Educational Psychology, 8, 293-316.

Paris, S. G.., Wasik, B. A., & Turner, J. C.. (1991). The development of strategic readers. In R. Barr, M. Kamil, P. Mosenthal, & P. D. Pearson (Eds.), Handbook of reading research, Vol. II (pp. 609-640). New York: Longman.

Snow, C. E., Burns, M. S., & Griffin, P. (Eds.) (1998). Preventing reading difficulties in young children. Washington, D. C.: National Academy Press.

Stanovich, K. E. (1992). Are we overselling literacy? In C. Temple & P. Collins (Eds.), Stories and readers: New perspectives on literature in the elementary classroom. Norwood, MA: Christopher Gordon.

Stein N. L. & Glenn, C. G. 1979. An analysis of story comprehension in elementary school children. In R. Freedle (Ed.), New directions in discourse processing. Norwood, NJ: Ablex. 53-120.

Stein N. L. & Nezworski, M. T. 1978. The effects of organization and instructional set on story memory. Discourse Processes, I, 177-193.

Wood, D. J., Bruner, J. S., & Ross, G. (1976). The role of tutoring in problem solving. Journal of Child Psychology and Psychiatry, 17, 89-100.

Notes

🐻 Success with California Content Standards

What We Are Doing in Class

We are working on these skills that address California English
Language Arts Content Standards:

Skills	California Content Standards
_____	_____
_____	_____
_____	_____
_____	_____

Your Child's Progress

Assessment in our classroom happens regularly. Here is my
most recent assessment data for your child.

Assessment Tool	Comments
_____	_____
_____	_____
_____	_____
_____	_____

Supporting Your Child

You are very important to your child's learning success. To help you, the
state of California has written a special booklet called *Parent Handbook
for English-Language Arts.* This publication provides information and
suggestions on how you can support your son or daughter's learning. It is
available for free at **www.cde.ca.gov/ls/pf/pf/documents/parentela.doc**

In addition, you will find specific information about the California Content
Standards and the English-Language Arts curriculum in the Reading-
Language Arts Framework for California Public Schools, K–12. Just go to
www.cde.ca.gov/re/pn/fd/documents/rlafw.pdf to download your free copy.